The Quick & Easy Spiralizer Cookbook

The
QUICK+EASY
Spiralizer Cookbook

100 Vegetable Noodle Recipes
You Can Make in 30 Minutes or Less

MEGAN FLYNN PETERSON

Photography by Marija Vidal

ROCKRIDGE
PRESS

To my daughter,
whom I hope to make proud.

Contents

 ## Snacks & Sides

Spiralized Quick Pickles 50

Baked Cinnamon Apple Chips 51

Spiralized Fruit Salad 52

Spiralized Sweet Potato Chips 53

Cucumber Noodle Salad with
Watermelon and Feta 54

Caprese Veggie Noodle Pasta Salad 55

Spiralized Potato Salad 56

Spiralized Veggie Spring Rolls 57

Spiralized Veggie Fritters 58

Spiralized Latkes 59

Vegan & Vegetarian Mains

Veggie Noodle Wraps 62

Cold Peanut Noodles 63

Chilled Sesame Noodles 64

Zucchini Noodles with Vegan
Avocado Cream Sauce 65

Greek Pasta Salad 66

Veggie Noodle Pasta Salad with
Goat Cheese, Almonds, and Cranberries 67

Potato Noodles with Mushrooms
and Sage 68

Lemon-Garlic Zucchini Noodles 69

Veggie Noodle Primavera 70

Zucchini Noodle Pomodoro 71

Cacio e Pepe 72

Veggie Pasta alla Norma 73

Fettuccini Alfredo 74

Lemony Broccoli Noodles with
Roasted Red Peppers 75

Vegan Veggie Noodle Mac and Cheese 76

Spiralized Potato Crust Pizza 77

 ## Fish & Seafood Mains

Ahi Tuna Steak over Chilled
Cucumber Noodles 80

Avocado and Crab Salad with
Cucumber Noodles 81

Thai Seafood Noodle Salad 82

Chilled Veggie Noodle Salad with
Asparagus and Shrimp 83

Pan-Roasted Salmon with
Lemon-Dill Squash Noodles 84

Black Pepper Daikon Noodles with
Shrimp and Snow Peas 85

Zucchini Noodle Puttanesca 86

Poached Tilapia over Veggie Noodles 87

Veggie Linguine with Clams 88

Spicy Shrimp Marinara 89

Lobster Mac and Cheese with
Butternut Squash Noodles 90

Summer Squash Pasta with
Lobster and Tomato 91

Seafood Veggie Pasta 92

Clam Chowder with Spiralized
Potatoes and Carrots 93

7 Chicken & Turkey Mains

8 Beef & Pork Mains

Introduction

When I gave up grains in 2012, I thought for sure the hardest thing to say goodbye to would be pasta. It was an easy dish and one that I absolutely loved, but after a few weeks of Paleo I realized that I didn't really miss noodles that much—I was enjoying so many whole foods and feeling incredibly satisfied on my new diet of meat, veggies, and fruit. The Paleo diet was working for me, and I wasn't planning on looking back.

Then one day almost a year later, to my delight, I discovered that you could cut a zucchini into noodles and prepare it like pasta. It was delicious and satisfying and added so many possibilities to my meals. Until that point, if I did find myself craving pasta, I would have some gluten-free noodles, which worked but overall made me feel like I was cheating on my Paleo diet. With zuc-chini noodles (or "zoodles," as they're sometimes called), I was able to satisfy my cravings and not stray from the tenets of Paleo, which made so much sense to me.

After discovering veggie noodles, I got a little handheld spiral veggie slicer, which worked perfectly on zucchini and carrots and even cucumbers. Once I was hooked, I wanted to expand my spiralizing repertoire, so I upgraded to a bigger spiralizer that stands on my kitchen counter and can spiralize virtually any veggie.

After four full years of Paleo, I started falling off the bandwagon a bit here and there, and finally in January 2017 decided to switch gears and give the keto diet a try. I love Paleo because it has worked so well for me—no grains, no dairy, no sugar. It's easy to learn, and once you get the hang of it you realize that it's not nearly as restrictive as it might seem at first glance. I feel so much better overall when I eat this way. Keto is great, too—it has a similar whole-foods focus, and spiralizing still fits in with this low-carb, high-fat lifestyle. I found it easy to lose weight and maintain optimal health by getting my macros in order. Eating a low-carb, high-fat diet gets your body into a state of ketosis, which helps you burn fat instead of sugar.

I've found that Paleo and keto are a great combination if you need that extra boost to lose a few pounds or jump-start your metab-olism. Keto is a bit more restrictive because you have to count calories, carbs, and fat, but once you get used to it, things become much more natural and meals become easy to plan—especially with the help of this cookbook as well as my previous ones! I like to think of keto as low-carb Paleo plus some dairy, which you can always substitute for if you're lactose intolerant. Getting enough fat is easy when you incorporate ingredients like coconut oil and avocado. If you'd like to learn more and give keto a try, you can easily find a keto calculator with a quick online search that will give you the right macros for your goals and body type. I'm excited about this book because it's the first place I've been able to combine Paleo and keto recipes, and I've even included some vegetarian and vegan dishes as well.

The year 2017 ended up being one of the busiest of my life—in addition to my blog, I was writing cookbooks like this one and studying to become a Pure Barre instructor. Getting healthy meals on the table for dinner every night was starting to become more of a challenge. A few months later I discovered I was pregnant with our first child, which (after a few months) made preparing healthy, Paleo-friendly, low-carb meals even more daunting. And that's where the idea was born (excuse the pun) for this book: a collection of recipes that use the spiralizer to get delicious, healthy, *and* fast meals on the table—because most of the time food should be all three of those things.

Incorporating a spiralizer into your meal planning is great because it makes veggies so much more fun and accessible, and it cuts down significantly on prep time. Cutting and chopping is always the slowest part of cooking for me, but with the spiralizer you can just pop a vegetable onto the machine, turn it a few times, and have a fully sliced ingredient, ready to go. I sometimes do all the veggies in a recipe as noodles, even if most of them are playing supporting roles (like onion and green pepper, and other aromatics like celery, carrots, etc.), because it's faster and easier than chopping everything with a knife.

In this cookbook you'll find recipes that can be prepped, cooked, and served within about 30 minutes. Many of the recipes require only five main ingredients (not counting a few basic pantry staples like cooking fats or spices), or they can be cooked in one pot, pan, or skillet. Some of them don't even require any cooking at all (they'll be labeled "No Cook" recipes and are mostly raw dishes or easy salads). The ingredients are natural, wholesome, and affordable—I'm not going to send you to any specialty stores to find ingredients that you'll use once and then stick in your pantry. Some of the recipes are Paleo, some are keto, all of them are gluten-free, some are dairy-free, and most importantly, all of them are satisfying and creatively use veggie noodles without sacrificing the familiar and delicious flavors that you love.

Chicken Pot Pie, *page 105*

1

Spiralized Meals Made Simple

This chapter will cover all the basics that you need to turn your spiralizer into a healthy meal-making machine. Sometimes getting an appliance like the spiralizer can be enough inspiration to get going, but I hope this book acts as an additional kick-starter for you to add veggies to dishes that would otherwise include not-so-healthy starches like pasta and rice.

Eat Your Vegetable Noodles

Veggie noodles have become increasingly popular over the past few years, and for good reason—they're an easy and tasty way to cut carbs, add variety to your meals, and get more nutrients into your diet every single day. With one simple piece of kitchen equipment, you can bring all kinds of dishes to life, and every one of them is centered around vegetables.

Convenient and Healthy

One of my favorite things about spiralizing, beyond how delicious veggie noodles can be, is how incredibly easy it makes meal prep. I will often spiralize an onion instead of chopping it on a cutting board because it is so much faster than using a knife. I try to spiralize a bunch of veggies at the beginning of the week and put them in separate containers so they're ready to go. They cook quickly, and many of them are also great raw, so having them pre-spiralized makes cooking and throwing salads together all week fast and easy. Here are a few ingredients that are super easy to spiralize and hold up well in the refrigerator:

- Zucchini (the perfect substitute for traditional pasta)

- Summer squash (a nice alternative to zucchini—sometimes harder to spiralize because of its shape, so look for larger ones that don't have much of a curve)

- Carrots (delicious when cooked, but also great as a crunchy raw noodle in salads)

- Onion (the perfect start to any dish)

- Cucumber (great for adding crunch to salads)

I find that in addition to substituting veggie noodles for carb-heavy staples like pasta or rice, I add more vegetables to my overall diet when I'm spiralizing. Having zucchini noodles or carrots ready to go often means that I'll add them to an omelet or a wrap that otherwise might have just been filled with meat and cheese.

How to Spiralize

Let's get into it! This next section is all about your spiralizer and some best practices for using it to its fullest potential.

An Overview of Spiralizers

There are a lot of different spiralizer brands and types on the market today, so you can take your pick when it comes to price and style. The most important thing about the spiralizers we'll use for this book is that they have easy-to-change blades, so you can switch up your noodles. Keeping food-related boredom at bay is kind of my thing, especially when it comes to veggies.

HAND-CRANK SPIRALIZERS

These spiralizers stand up on your counter, and you turn a handle to slice the noodles. Unlike hourglass spiralizers, these spiralize more than just long and round veggies—you can do beets, onions, parsnips, apples, and so much more. If you can peel it and fit it on the machine, you can make noodles out of it!

They're relatively inexpensive and easy to clean, but they are a bit large and take up some space in your kitchen. The blades are incredibly sharp, so you want to make sure you always handle them with care! It's only happened once, but I have sliced my thumb on mine and it wasn't a great experience.

I use the Inspiralizer brand, but there's also Paderno, SpiraLife, Brieftons, and many more. The blades may differ in some minor ways, but overall, they have the same offerings. There's usually a big ribbon noodle, a classic spaghetti noodle, and one or two different-size pastas like fettuccini or linguine. Most of the time they're labeled A, B, or C (and D, depending on what brand you own), and each of the recipes in this book calls out a specific blade to use, although you can use whichever one you like if you decide you have a favorite. I like using the ribbon blade for sautéed dishes and salads, the fettuccini and linguine blades for more traditional pasta substitutions, and the spaghetti blade when I'm really trying to cut down on cook time (it yields the thinnest noodle, so it makes quick work of softening hardy vegetables like sweet potato or butternut squash).

How to Use: Hand-crank spiralizers vary by brand, but generally you will set them down on your counter and attach the veggie you plan to spiralize to the side of the machine with the blade. Then you slide the hand-crank over to secure the vegetable in place and turn the handle to create veggie noodles.

Pros:
- Much sturdier than the hourglass model
- Can spiralize virtually any fruit or vegetable
- Has an assortment of blades for variety in noodle shape and size

Cons:
- More expensive
- Takes up more space in kitchen/storage
- Takes a little practice to master

HOURGLASS SPIRALIZERS

If you aren't sure you want to invest in one of the hand-crank spiralizer brands (they're bigger machines that stand up on your counter), you can always start out with a cone-shaped handheld spiralizer like the Veggetti.

How to Use: Hold the hourglass spiralizer with one hand and place the vegetable into the cone with your other hand, turning it to slice noodles. Most of the time these spiralizers have two size options, so you can make a thicker noodle or a thinner one depending on which side of the hourglass you choose.

Pros:
- Smaller
- Cheaper
- Easier to use/learn
- Less of a space and/or budget commitment

Cons:
- Limited function
- Not as long-lasting

A handheld hourglass spiralizer, while cheaper and space-saving, is going to limit you to veggies that fit in it—zucchini, cucumber, carrots, and that's about it. Your vegetables need to be long and round, so onions, turnips, and any other noncylindrical veggies are not going to work.

A FEW WORDS ON CLEANING

I like to spiralize a bunch of vegetables at once and then give the spiralizer a good cleaning. I use a brush, dish soap, and hot water and carefully scrub the whole thing to make sure I get any veggie bits out of the blades. Just be careful when handling the spiralizer—the blades are sharp!

Spiralizer Blades

The recipes in this book mostly use spaghetti or linguine noodles, as well as ribbon noodles for salads and a few of the casseroles. My spiralizer has the blades labeled as follows:

Blade A: Ribbon noodles—very wide and flat

Blade B: Fettuccini—wide and flat

Blade C: Linguine—semi-wide and round

Blade D: Spaghetti—round and thin

You may need to consult your manual to see which noodle and blade is which. Make sure to spend some time experimenting to figure out which ones are your favorites. For a long time I thought blade D was my favorite, but now my go-to is blade C.

Keep in mind that different-size noodles will have different cooking times—ribbon noodles (A) will cook much quicker than linguine (C) or spaghetti (D). You can pick a favorite and stick with it, but this book is going to have you switching it up a lot.

What to Spiralize

Choosing Spiral-Friendly Produce

You can spiralize almost any veggie, but there are some that work exceptionally well with a spiralizer.

In addition to the classics like zucchini, cucumbers, potatoes, and broccoli, you can also spiralize veggies like onions and even fruit such as apples and pears. Shop around and experiment. The best fruits and veggies for spiralizing don't have hollow centers, a bunch of seeds, or tough cores (there are a few exceptions to this—you can easily spiralize a pineapple or a butternut squash), and they're at least a few inches thick and long so you have something to actually spiralize. You also want something with a solid flesh that isn't going to fall apart under pressure— think apples over peaches.

Minimizing Waste

Spiralizing is a great way to use up veggies, but there are often lots of bits and pieces that get left behind. One of my favorite things to do with leftover cores and pieces of veggies that don't make it into noodles is to add them to a bag in the freezer and save them for broth. I save onion skins, carrot peels, and pretty much any veggie pieces that fall off while spiralizing. When the bag is full, I add the scraps to a pot with a garlic clove or two and cover with water, then bring it to a low simmer for an hour or two (veggie broth shouldn't cook for a long time the way bone broth does or it'll get kind of bitter).

My Top 15 Spiralizable Produce

PRODUCE	HOW TO PREPARE	COOKING METHOD	BEST WAY TO EAT	BLADE TYPE
Zucchini	Trim ends; no need to peel.	Raw or lightly sautéed	Noodles, soups	B, C, or D
Summer Squash	Trim ends; no need to peel.	Raw or lightly sautéed	Noodles, soups	B, C, or D
Beets	Peel and trim ends.	Raw or lightly sautéed	Salads	Any
Carrots	Use medium-large carrots. Peel and trim ends.	Raw or lightly sautéed	Noodles, soups, salads	Any
Butternut Squash	Peel very thoroughly, cut bulb off, and spiralize only top of vegetable (part without seeds).	Roasted or sautéed	Noodles, soups, casseroles	A, B, or C
Sweet Potatoes	Peel and trim ends.	Roasted or sautéed	Noodles, soups, casseroles, salads	Any
White Potatoes	Peel if desired. Trim ends before spiralizing.	Roasted or sautéed	Noodles, casseroles, as a crust or sandwich	Any
Cucumbers	Peel if desired. Trim ends before spiralizing.	Raw	Salads	Any
Broccoli	Remove florets, and peel stem to remove any bumps/knots. Spiralize stem only.	Lightly sautéed or roasted	Noodles, soups, stir-fry	B, C, or D
Turnips	Peel and trim ends.	Roasted or sautéed	Noodles, casseroles	C or D
Cabbage	Trim side without stem; use stem to anchor to spiralizer.	Raw, roasted, or sautéed	Salads, stir-fry	A
Bell Peppers	Trim stem and remove seeds before spiralizing.	Raw or lightly sautéed	Noodles, stir-fry, salads	D
Onions	Trim ends; remove papery outer layers.	Roasted or sautéed	Great in everything as an aromatic	D
Daikon Radish	Peel and trim ends.	Roasted or sautéed	Noodles, rice, stir-fry	C or D
Apples	Seed with a corer and trim ends.	Raw or lightly sautéed	Salads, baked dishes	A

Tips for Spiralizing Successfully

Any time you get a new kitchen appliance there can be a bit of a learning curve, and especially with spiralizing, where you're generally making significant changes to your diet as well. Here are a few tips to make spiralizing a breeze:

- Try to find veggies that are easy to spiralize. This will get easier as you gain experience, but for starters you want to make sure the vegetable is thick enough to give you something to spiralize and straight enough that you actually get noodles from it.

- Wash and peel your vegetables before spiralizing. Things like zucchini or potatoes don't need to be peeled unless you prefer it, but vegetables that you'd usually peel should be peeled before you turn them into noodles (e.g., sweet potatoes, carrots, or onions).

- Dry noodles before cooking them to prevent sogginess. If you're working with zucchini or summer squash, and you have a little extra time, I recommend letting them sweat in a colander for at least 20 minutes with 2 to 3 tablespoons of salt sprinkled over them. After 20 minutes, give them a rinse, pat them dry, and continue with your recipe. It adds some prep time, but if you get used to it and plan ahead, you can always have them ready to go. This step is optional, of course. If you are pressed for time or don't want the extra mess, just cook your zucchini or squash noodles a little less—2 to 3 minutes at the most—to keep the noodles al dente, with a texture that mimics traditional pasta.

- Trim veggie noodles after spiralizing—otherwise you're going to have a few super-long noodles. I like to go through with scissors and cut them up roughly to create noodles that are a little more manageable in length.

Helpful Kitchen Equipment

So, you have your spiralizer and you're ready to dive into the world of veggie noodles! There are a few pieces of kitchen equipment that will make cooking this way even easier for you. Spiralizing is super quick and simple, but it does take a bit of prep. The following items will make prepping, spiralizing, and cooking healthy meals a breeze.

Must Have

Good knives: A sharp, quality chef's knife and paring knife are important for trimming veggies before putting them on the spiralizer and chopping other ingredients quickly and safely. Be sure to sharpen your knives regularly or have them sharpened professionally.

Cutting boards: Choose wood or plastic, and make sure your board is wide enough to easily cut large produce items like butternut squash. I love the look of wooden cutting boards (especially a big, beautiful one I can leave on my counter), but I find that plastic ones are a lot more useable because you can cut veggies and raw meat on them and they clean up a little more easily. If you're looking for just one, I'd go with a nice big plastic one.

Good peeler: Many vegetables (butternut squash, carrots, etc.) should be peeled before you slice them on the spiralizer. Find a peeler with a sturdy, sharp blade that fits comfortably in your hand.

Handheld or box grater for "ricing" or shredding veggies: Cauliflower is a great low-carb substitution for rice and even some breads, but it doesn't spiralize well, so I use a grater to shred it into a rice-like consistency before cooking.

Large nonstick skillet or pan: Essential for sautéing veggie noodles.

Heavy, medium to large stockpot: Necessary for quickly boiling veggie noodles or making more complex dishes like soups and stews.

Nice to Have

Blender or food processor: This will make ricing or shredding veggies much easier than a handheld or box grater, but it's not necessary at all.

Slow cooker: It's not the best choice for cooking veggie noodles, but you can easily cook a dish in the slow cooker all day and toss the noodles in a few minutes before serving.

Pantry Essentials

Veggies and proteins are important, but a well-stocked pantry can make healthy cooking much easier and more delicious. These are basic spices and pantry items that I always have in the cupboard and refrigerator to enhance the flavor of my meals:

- Coconut oil
- Dried herbs and spices (my most-used are garlic powder, onion powder, red pepper flakes, cayenne pepper, oregano, and thyme)
- Eggs (pasture-raised whenever possible)
- Extra-virgin olive oil
- Ghee (if you can't find this in the store, there's a recipe on page 19)
- Gluten-free soy sauce (or coconut aminos if strict Paleo)
- Grass-fed butter
- Honey (or agave nectar if vegan)
- Hot sauce (I love Frank's RedHot and Sriracha)
- Kosher salt
- Peppercorns (I highly recommend using fresh-ground pepper!)
- Rice vinegar
- Toasted sesame oil

These are just the basics that I always have around, but you'll also occasionally find curry powder or chili-garlic sauce in my pantry. Pick your favorites and stock up on them so you're always ready to cook something delicious!

Five Low-Carb Substitute Staples

As you now know, spiralized veggie noodles can be a game changer when it comes to adding variety to a lower-carb diet. The following five vegetables are the ones I use the most when substituting for things like pasta, rice, and even bread:

1. Zucchini
2. Summer squash
3. Daikon radish
4. Cauliflower
5. Broccoli

PASTA

My favorite substitution for pasta is the classic zucchini noodle, or "zoodle." When time permits, I make sure to salt the zoodles really well and let them sit in a colander in the sink for at least 20 minutes—this helps remove any excess moisture, which keeps them from getting soggy during the cooking process. I also only cook them for a few minutes—just long enough to get incorporated into whatever sauce, seasoning, and/or protein I'm cooking them with. I think preserving that crunch really helps mimic an al dente pasta texture, which is so important. I also love using summer squash instead of zucchini because it has an even milder flavor, and since it's white or yellow instead of green, it often looks even more like regular noodles.

RICE

You can make low-carb "rice" by spiralizing a firm vegetable like daikon radish and then chopping it up or throwing it in the food processor until it's the consistency of rice. You can also make cauliflower into "rice" by grating it with a handheld grater, tossing it in the food processor, or even buying pre-riced cauliflower from the produce section of your favorite grocery store. There's a recipe for fried rice on page 124, but you can make an even simpler version by sautéing it in butter or olive oil over medium-high heat for 8 to 10 minutes and seasoning with salt and pepper. It's great with almost any sauce or protein or even by itself for a quick snack.

BREAD

My mom blew my mind about a year ago when she made delicious little bread-like rounds out of cauliflower and broccoli in the oven. I like to make a batch and use them for sandwiches when I'm in the mood for something like that. You can find a recipe on page 23. It starts with riced cauliflower, which you can buy pre-made. I almost always use the Trader Joe's brand, but the pieces are a little too big, so I like to give it a quick spin in the food processor. Whether you purchase it or make it yourself, aim for pieces the size of rice grains for best results.

About the Recipes

The recipes in this book are meant to be both straightforward and delicious—my goal is for you to be able to get a healthy meal on the table in about 30 minutes or less without having to spend a ton of time or money at the grocery store. Every recipe in this book can be prepared quickly from readily available ingredients, and at least half of these recipes are labeled "5-Ingredient," "No Cook," or "One Pot."

- 5-Ingredient: Recipe uses 5 or fewer ingredients, not including cooking fats or spices.

- No Cook: Fast, easy recipe that doesn't require cooking, such as a salad or raw noodle dish.

- One Pot: Recipe can be prepped and cooked in one pot, pan, or bowl. Fewer dishes means more time to eat and more time to spend doing other things you love!

You'll also find nutritional information and diet labels. I've included some variations to meet specific dietary needs as well, so you can swap out certain ingredients to make something Paleo or vegan. When it comes to the recipes labeled Keto, you'll want to consider how many carbs you're consuming with other meals and snacks throughout the day. A keto calculator can help you figure out the ideal carb/protein/fat ratio for your personal goals. Every recipe in this book is gluten-free, and each recipe is labeled as follows so you can easily identify what works with your personal dietary preferences and restrictions:

- Dairy-Free
- Keto
- Paleo
- Vegan
- Vegetarian

Paleo Carrot Noodle Banana Bread Muffins, *page 14*

Breakfast & Brunch

Breakfast was my least favorite meal of the day when I was a kid, but now that I'm an adult I have to say it may be my favorite. I love going out for brunch or making a big breakfast at home, especially on the weekend. I usually do eggs, bacon, sometimes a potato or two, and always plenty of coffee— but until I started spiralizing, I never really thought of ways to incorporate many vegetables into my breakfasts and/or brunches. This chapter is full of breakfast recipes that will hopefully help you add more veggies into your first (and most important, they say!) meal of the day.

Spiralized Fruit Smoothie Bowl

5-INGREDIENT • NO COOK • PALEO • VEGAN

I'm a huge fan of smoothies in the morning, but they can get kind of boring day after day. I love making a smoothie bowl when I have time to sit down and eat it because I can top it with a variety of fruits, nuts, and seeds to make it both satisfying to eat and beautiful to look at. This recipe is for one of my favorite smoothie bowls, and I've incorporated my favorite toppings, but you can easily customize it to make it your own.

Serves 2
Prep time: 10 minutes
Blade: A, B, or C

2 cups frozen berries

2 bananas

1 cup fresh spinach

1 cup almond milk

Toppings: spiralized apple, pear, even orange (you can spiralize it with the peel on using blade A); sliced almonds; unsweetened coconut; chia seeds

1. In a blender, purée the berries, bananas, spinach, and almond milk until smooth.

2. Pour into two bowls, add your desired toppings, and serve.

TIP: If you aren't vegan and want to add some dairy, you can add ½ to 1 cup of yogurt to the smoothie mixture.

PER SERVING Calories: 230; Saturated Fat: 0g; Total Fat: 4g; Protein: 4g; Total Carbs: 46g; Fiber: 10g; Sodium: 193mg

Zucchini Noodle Oatmeal

5-INGREDIENT • ONE POT • VEGAN

Since I eat a mostly Paleo diet, I don't often have oatmeal, but whenever I do I always love it and go through a big oatmeal phase, eating it almost every morning. It's so easy and filling, and you can customize it a hundred different ways. This recipe sneaks zucchini in, which might sound strange, but I find it's a great way to get some extra vegetables into your (or your kids') diet.

Serves 4
Prep time: 5 minutes
Cook time: 5 minutes
Blade: B

3½ cups water

¼ teaspoon salt

2 cups quick-cooking oats

1 large zucchini, spiralized and roughly chopped

Flavor enhancers (optional): 1 teaspoon vanilla extract, 1 teaspoon ground cinnamon, ¼ cup raisins, sliced bananas, sliced almonds, and/or a few tablespoons peanut butter

1. In a medium saucepan, bring the water and salt to a boil.

2. Add the oats, and reduce the heat to low. Simmer uncovered for 1 minute, stirring occasionally. Remove from the heat and let stand, covered, for about 1 minute to allow the oats to absorb the remaining liquid.

3. Add the zucchini to the oats, and stir well to combine. Spoon into serving bowls, garnish with desired toppings, and serve.

TIP: Cook the oats in your favorite dairy or plant milk for even more flavor.

PER SERVING Calories: 163; Saturated Fat: 1g; Total Fat: 3g; Protein: 6g; Total Carbs: 29g; Fiber: 5g; Sodium: 155mg

Paleo Carrot Noodle Banana Bread Muffins

PALEO • VEGETARIAN

If you're anything like me, you buy bananas and then forget about them on a regular basis. It's an annoying habit, but it does mean one good thing: banana bread! I used to make this recipe in a loaf pan, but muffins cook faster and are perfect for meal prep. There's nothing easier than grabbing a delicious muffin on your way out the door in the morning. The carrot noodles add some extra nutrition and help me use up leftover carrots in my refrigerator, which I forget about almost as often as I do the bananas.

Makes 12 muffins
Prep time: 5 minutes
Cook time: 25 minutes
Blade: D

3 or 4 very ripe bananas, mashed until smooth

4 large eggs

½ cup almond butter

4 tablespoons (½ stick) grass-fed butter, melted

1 teaspoon vanilla extract

½ cup coconut flour

1 teaspoon baking soda

1 teaspoon baking powder

1 teaspoon ground cinnamon

Pinch salt

2 or 3 carrots, spiralized

1. Preheat the oven to 375°F. Line a muffin tin with baking cups.

2. In a large bowl, stir the bananas, eggs, almond butter, butter, and vanilla until well combined.

3. Add the coconut flour, baking soda, baking powder, cinnamon, and salt. Mix well and gently fold in the carrots.

4. Spoon the batter evenly into the muffin cups and bake for 20 to 25 minutes, or until a knife or toothpick inserted into the center of a muffin comes out clean.

5. Serve immediately, or refrigerate in a covered container for up to 5 days.

TIP: Make these muffins into more of a dessert by mixing in ½ cup of dark-chocolate chips or chunks.

PER SERVING (1 muffin) Calories: 142; Saturated Fat: 4g; Total Fat: 7g; Protein: 4g; Total Carbs: 16g; Fiber: 5g; Sodium: 195mg

Spiralized Zucchini Bread Muffins

PALEO • VEGETARIAN

I like making these muffins in the fall and winter to enjoy as a simple breakfast with a cup of coffee, or maybe even an afternoon snack with hot tea. Spiralizing the zucchini is faster than shredding, and it makes the muffins a little more exciting—who doesn't want zucchini noodles in their zucchini bread? You really can put veggie noodles in everything—even baked goods!

Makes 12 muffins
Prep time: 5 minutes
Cook time: 25 minutes
Blade: D

¾ cup coconut flour

6 large eggs

½ cup pure maple syrup or agave nectar

¼ cup coconut oil or grass-fed butter, melted

1 teaspoon vanilla extract

1 teaspoon ground cinnamon

¾ teaspoon baking soda

Pinch salt

1 large zucchini, spiralized

1. Preheat the oven to 375°F. Line a muffin tin with baking cups.

2. In a large bowl, combine the coconut flour, eggs, maple syrup, coconut oil, vanilla, cinnamon, baking soda, and salt. Stir well, then add the zucchini noodles, tossing gently to incorporate.

3. Spoon the batter evenly into the muffin cups and bake for 20 to 25 minutes, or until a knife or toothpick inserted into the center of a muffin comes out clean. Remove from the oven and cool before popping them out of the tins.

4. Serve immediately, or refrigerate in a covered container for up to 5 days.

TIP: If you have more time and want to make this into a loaf of bread instead of muffins, pour the batter into a small loaf pan and bake for 40 to 45 minutes or until a knife or toothpick inserted into the center of the loaf comes out clean.

PER SERVING Calories: 180; Saturated Fat: 5g; Total Fat: 9g; Protein: 7g; Total Carbs: 19g; Fiber: 6g; Sodium: 187mg

Grain-Free Spiralized Apple Pancakes

PALEO · VEGETARIAN

I originally made this recipe with bacon instead of apple noodles, but when fall comes around I crave the combination of apples and cinnamon and find myself putting them in every dish I possibly can. This pancake recipe is simple to prepare, and the pancakes flip relatively easily, which can sometimes be a challenge when you aren't working with conventional flour. I love them topped with some butter and a little bit of warmed maple syrup, but if you're watching your carbs you can always skip the syrup.

Serves 2 to 4
Prep time: 5 minutes
Cook time: 15 minutes
Blade: A or D

2 ripe bananas

3 large eggs

3 tablespoons coconut flour

1 teaspoon vanilla extract

¼ teaspoon baking soda

½ teaspoon ground cinnamon

Pinch salt

1 to 2 tablespoons grass-fed butter, plus more for topping

1 large apple, spiralized

A few tablespoons pure maple syrup, for topping (optional)

1. In a blender or food processor, process the bananas, eggs, coconut flour, vanilla, baking soda, cinnamon, and salt until smooth.

2. On a griddle or in a large nonstick skillet over medium heat, melt some of the butter. Spoon small, flat piles of apple noodles, about the size of your palm, onto the cooking surface, leaving enough space between them to easily flip the pancakes. Allow to cook for 1 to 2 minutes.

3. Once the noodles have softened slightly, pour a small amount of the pancake batter over each pile of apples, creating a round pancake. Cook for 3 to 4 minutes and flip carefully, cooking for another 3 to 4 minutes on the other side. Remove from the heat and keep warm. Repeat with the remaining butter, apples, and batter.

4. Serve hot with a bit more butter or a drizzle of maple syrup (if using).

TIP: Try using bacon instead of apples if you aren't a vegetarian and want to add some extra fat and protein to this recipe.

PER SERVING Calories: 472; Saturated Fat: 13g; Total Fat: 22g; Protein: 15g; Total Carbs: 57g; Fiber: 15g; Sodium: 458mg

Paleo Crêpes with Pear Noodles

PALEO • VEGETARIAN

I'm more of a savory breakfast person, but when I'm in the mood for a sweeter breakfast or brunch, these Paleo crêpes hit the spot every time. I love filling them with a nice fruit and honey reduction, and the pear noodles are just delicious wrapped up in warm, fluffy (and grain-free!) crêpes.

Serves 2
Prep time: 5 minutes
Cook time: 20 minutes
Blade: D

FOR THE PEAR NOODLES

1 tablespoon grass-fed butter

1 large pear, spiralized

Juice of ½ lemon

1 to 2 tablespoons honey (optional)

FOR THE CRÊPES

5 large eggs

3 tablespoons almond flour

2 tablespoons arrowroot powder (sifted to remove lumps)

1 teaspoon vanilla extract

1 teaspoon ground cinnamon

Pinch salt

2 tablespoons coconut oil or grass-fed butter, for greasing the pan

TO MAKE THE PEAR NOODLES

1. In a large nonstick skillet over medium heat, melt the butter. Add the pear noodles, lemon juice, and honey (if using). Stir gently to combine, and sauté for 2 to 3 minutes.

2. Reduce the heat to low and cover.

TO MAKE THE CRÊPES

1. In a medium bowl, whisk the eggs. Add the almond flour, arrowroot powder, vanilla, cinnamon, and salt. Mix well to combine.

2. Heat a medium nonstick skillet over medium heat. Add some of the coconut oil to the pan, then quickly pour in about ¼ cup of crêpe batter. Tilt the pan to spread the batter in an even layer, and cook for 2 to 3 minutes, until the underside is golden brown.

3. Flip the crêpe with a large spatula, and cook for about a minute more until golden brown on the bottom.

4. Transfer to a plate, keep warm, and repeat with the remaining oil and batter.

5. Remove the pear noodles from the heat. Assemble the crêpes by adding a few tablespoons of pear to the middle of each crêpe, then roll up and serve immediately.

TIP: Use apples instead of pears for a flavor variation.

PER SERVING Calories: 432; Saturated Fat: 19g; Total Fat: 32g; Protein: 15g; Total Carbs: 22g; Fiber: 3g; Sodium: 279mg

Sweet Potato Noodle Hash Browns

5-INGREDIENT • ONE POT • PALEO • VEGETARIAN

I used to make this sweet potato hash brown recipe all the time when we had people over for brunch, but I stopped after a while because peeling and chopping always takes me so long, and if I forget to do it ahead of time I end up just not doing it at all. Spiralizing all the ingredients makes it twice as fast, so now I make these sweet potato noodle hash browns more often than ever!

Serves 1 or 2
Prep time: 5 minutes
Cook time: 20 minutes
Blade: C

2 garlic cloves, chopped

1 small onion, spiralized

½ green bell pepper, spiralized and roughly chopped

2 tablespoons ghee (or clarified grass-fed butter), divided

2 medium sweet potatoes, peeled and spiralized

Salt

Freshly ground black pepper

¼ teaspoon red pepper flakes (optional)

Chopped scallions, for garnish (optional)

1. In a large skillet over medium-high heat, sauté the garlic, onions, and green pepper with 1 tablespoon of ghee for 5 to 7 minutes, or until the onion becomes translucent and the peppers have softened slightly.

2. Add the sweet potato noodles and the remaining 1 tablespoon of ghee and stir well to combine. Continue to cook, stirring occasionally, for 10 to 15 minutes, or until the sweet potato noodles are golden brown and beginning to develop a slight crispiness around the edges. Season with salt, pepper, and the red pepper flakes (if using).

3. Remove from the heat, garnish with the scallions (if using), and serve immediately.

TIP: Make this recipe dairy-free by swapping ghee for olive or coconut oil. If you can't find ghee or clarified butter in a store, it's easy to make at home:

1. In a heavy-bottomed saucepan, melt about a pound of grass-fed, unsalted butter (cut into chunks or squares) over medium heat, stirring occasionally.

2. Once the butter comes to a simmer, turn the heat down to medium-low and allow it to bubble for 5 to 6 minutes. There should be foam on top as the milk solids start to curdle and attach to the sides of the pan. Eventually the milk solids will drop to the bottom of the pan and the butter will foam again.

3. At that point, remove from the heat, allow to settle for a few minutes, and then strain the melted butter through cheesecloth.

4. Discard the solids left behind, and pour the clarified butter into a jar. Let sit for several hours at room temperature to solidify before refrigerating.

PER SERVING Calories: 548; Saturated Fat: 18g; Total Fat: 28g; Protein: 6g; Total Carbs: 69g; Fiber: 11g; Sodium: 305mg

Veggie Noodle Omelet

5-INGREDIENT · DAIRY-FREE · KETO · PALEO · VEGETARIAN

This easy omelet is a great choice for a busy weekday morning. I love spiralizing veggies instead of cutting them up because not only are they more fun to eat, they also take much less time to prep and cook. It's perfect when you're trying to get out the door but still want to eat something healthy and filling before you go. You could always add ham or bacon to this omelet if you wanted some meat, but eggs and veggies together are an incredibly satisfying (and vegetarian) way to start the day.

Serves 2
Prep time: 5 minutes
Cook time: 20 minutes
Blade: D

½ onion, spiralized

1 garlic clove, minced

2 tablespoons olive oil, divided

1 medium zucchini, spiralized

1 medium carrot, spiralized

Salt

Freshly ground black pepper

4 large eggs

1. In a large nonstick skillet over medium-high heat, sauté the onion and garlic together in 1 tablespoon of olive oil for 3 minutes.

2. Add the zucchini and carrot noodles, and stir to combine. Sauté for an additional 4 to 5 minutes, or until the vegetables have softened slightly. Season with salt and pepper. Remove everything from the pan and set aside.

3. In a small bowl, whisk the eggs. Heat ½ tablespoon of the remaining olive oil in the pan you sautéed the vegetables in over medium heat. Pour half of the whisked eggs into the pan and tilt the pan around to spread the eggs in a thin, even layer.

4. Cook for 2 to 3 minutes until the egg has set, then flip and add half of the spiralized zucchini and carrot. Season with salt and pepper, fold the omelet in half, and transfer to a plate. Repeat with the remaining ½ tablespoon of olive oil and the remaining egg and veggies.

5. Serve hot.

TIP: Make this recipe a little more keto-friendly by adding ½ cup of shredded cheese.

PER SERVING Calories: 304; Saturated Fat: 5g; Total Fat: 24g; Protein: 14g; Total Carbs: 10g; Fiber: 3g; Sodium: 250mg

Eggs Benedict over Potato Noodle "English Muffins"

PALEO

I've been working on my recipe for homemade eggs Benedict for a few years now, and every time I tweak it I think it gets a little better. When I'm feeling lazy, I use sliced tomatoes as a base. This recipe uses potato noodles to create gluten-free "English muffins." It's so good, and worth that little bit of extra effort.

Serves 4
Prep time: 10 minutes
Cook time: 20 minutes
Blade: D

FOR THE POTATO "ENGLISH MUFFINS"

2 tablespoons olive oil, divided

1 large russet potato, spiralized

1 large egg, beaten

Salt

Freshly ground black pepper

FOR THE EGGS AND HOLLANDAISE SAUCE

Splash white vinegar

8 whole large eggs, plus 4 large egg yolks for the Hollandaise sauce

2 tablespoons olive oil

4 thick-cut ham or Canadian bacon slices

1 tablespoon freshly squeezed lemon juice

8 tablespoons (1 stick) unsalted, grass-fed butter, melted

¼ teaspoon cayenne pepper

Pinch salt

Freshly ground black pepper

TO MAKE THE POTATO "ENGLISH MUFFINS"

1. In a large skillet over medium-high heat, heat the olive oil. Sauté the potato noodles for 4 to 5 minutes, or until softened. Transfer to a medium bowl, cool slightly, and toss with the egg. Season with salt and pepper.

2. Transfer the mixture to four ramekins or round cookie cutters (about 5-inch diameter), pressing down slightly to pack them in. Pop them into the refrigerator for a few minutes to set.

TO MAKE THE EGGS AND HOLLANDAISE SAUCE

1. While the "muffins" are setting, bring a large saucepan of water to a low simmer. Add the white vinegar.

2. Crack 1 egg into a small bowl. Use a large spoon to swirl the water into a slow whirlpool. Carefully drop the egg into the water and, without hitting the egg, continue the swirling motion with the spoon. Allow to cook for a minute or two until the whites have set. Carefully scoop the egg out and place it on a paper towel. Repeat with the remaining 7 whole eggs.

3. Remove the "muffins" from the refrigerator. In a large skillet over medium-high heat, fry them in the olive oil for 3 to 4 minutes per side until lightly browned. Remove from the heat and set aside.

4. In the skillet you used for the potato, heat the ham over medium-high heat for about 2 minutes until warmed through.

➤

5. To make the Hollandaise sauce, in a heat-proof bowl, quickly whisk the egg yolks and lemon juice together until the mixture becomes frothy and starts to expand. Place the bowl over a pot of simmering water (don't let the bowl touch the water) and continue to whisk. Slowly drizzle the melted butter in while stirring, and continue to whisk until the sauce has doubled in size.

6. Remove from the heat, add the cayenne and salt, and season with pepper. Serve immediately or keep warm until ready to serve.

7. To assemble the eggs Benedict, plate the potato noodle cake, add a slice of ham, then top with the poached egg and Hollandaise.

TIP: Once you get the hang of it, you can poach several eggs at a time—just keep some space between each egg as you add them. Make this a keto recipe by skipping the potato noodle "English muffin" and using a handful of spinach instead.

PER SERVING Calories: 598; Saturated Fat: 22g; Total Fat: 54g; Protein: 22g; Total Carbs: 9g; Fiber: 1g; Sodium: 754mg

Bacon, Egg, and Cheese on Cauliflower Bread

KETO

This cauliflower bread takes a few extra minutes, but it's a staple in my house because it is such a great substitution for regular bread, and I really enjoy sandwiches. Try making a double batch and storing half to reheat on busy mornings. I love a bacon, egg, and cheese sandwich on the weekends, and it's even better when it's gluten-free and grain-free. If you eat Paleo or don't tolerate dairy, just skip the cheese on this sandwich.

Serves 2
Prep time: 10 minutes
Cook time: 20 minutes

FOR THE CAULIFLOWER BREAD

1 head cauliflower

3 large eggs

1 shallot, minced

1 teaspoon dried oregano

1 teaspoon chopped
fresh chives

1 teaspoon chopped
fresh parsley

3 garlic cloves, chopped

1 teaspoon salt

Freshly ground black pepper

FOR THE SANDWICHES

2 large eggs

½ tablespoon
grass-fed butter

2 Cheddar cheese slices

4 cooked bacon slices

Salt

Freshly ground black pepper

TO MAKE THE CAULIFLOWER BREAD

1. Preheat the oven to 350°F.

2. In a food processor, pulse the cauliflower until the pieces resemble grains of rice. Transfer to a microwave-safe bowl and cook on high in the microwave for 2 minutes. Allow to cool for a few minutes, then twist in a thin cloth or cheesecloth to remove any water (not a lot will come out, but the little that's there needs to be removed). If you don't have a food processor, you can use a box grater to shred the cauliflower.

3. Transfer the cauliflower to a medium bowl. In a smaller bowl, whisk the eggs together with the shallot, oregano, chives, parsley, garlic, salt, and a few twists of pepper. Pour the mixture over the cauliflower, and stir together until well incorporated.

4. Line a large baking sheet with parchment paper or aluminum foil. Scoop on the cauliflower mixture in four equal parts, then spread them out until each is about a ¼-inch thick, with a little room in between. Bake for 10 minutes, then flip and bake for another 7 minutes.

5. Remove from the oven and allow to cool slightly.

➤

TO MAKE THE SANDWICHES

1. In a small bowl, whisk the eggs.

2. In a large nonstick skillet over medium-high heat, melt the butter. Pour the eggs in and spread with a heat-proof spatula to create an even layer of egg, then cook for 2 minutes, or until the egg mixture is set. Reduce the heat to medium-low and cut the egg into two pieces in the pan. Flip each piece and add a slice of cheese to each.

3. Assemble the sandwiches by layering two pieces of cauli-flower bread with cheesy egg and 2 bacon slices each. Season with salt and pepper, top with another piece of cauliflower bread, and serve immediately.

TIP: Make a double batch of the bread for later. (Store in the refrigerator.) To reheat, broil quickly in the oven or toaster oven. Multitask this recipe to keep it under 30 minutes. Pop the cauliflower bread into the oven, then prepare the eggs while it's baking. If you don't have a microwave, cook the riced cauli-flower in a dry nonstick skillet for a few minutes, then proceed with the recipe.

PER SERVING Calories: 569; Saturated Fat: 17g; Total Fat: 41g; Protein: 40g; Total Carbs: 12g; Fiber: 4g; Sodium: 2451mg

Baked Eggs in Sweet Potato Noodle Nests

5-INGREDIENT • ONE POT • DAIRY-FREE • PALEO • VEGETARIAN

Baked eggs are one of my favorite breakfast and brunch recipes because they feel kind of fancy, but they're super easy to make. If I'm having people over or just want to make a nice breakfast on a weekend, I like to crack a few eggs into a ramekin with some cream and bake them slowly until the whites have set. This recipe is even easier to make in larger batches because you use a muffin tin, and I've added sweet potato "nests" to hold each egg and make the dish a little more substantial.

Serves 2 to 4
Prep time: 5 minutes
Cook time: 20 minutes
Blade: D

1 large sweet potato, peeled and spiralized
1 tablespoon olive oil
Salt
Freshly ground black pepper
4 large eggs

1. Preheat the oven to 400°F.

2. In a large bowl, toss the sweet potato noodles with the olive oil, and season with salt and pepper.

3. Divide the sweet potato noodles into four and press into four cups of a muffin tin. Bake for 5 minutes.

4. Reduce the oven temperature to 375°F. Crack an egg into each sweet potato "nest" and season with more salt and pepper. Bake for 10 to 15 minutes until the noodles are softened and the egg is no longer runny (or cooked to your desired consistency).

5. Remove from the oven and allow to cool slightly before serving.

TIP: If you like to incorporate more meat into your breakfasts, add some chopped bacon to each egg. This will give you a little more fat as well, making this a more keto-friendly recipe.

PER SERVING Calories: 259; Saturated Fat: 4g; Total Fat: 17g; Protein: 14g; Total Carbs: 14g; Fiber: 2g; Sodium: 253mg

Skillet Spiralized Egg Hash

5-INGREDIENT · DAIRY-FREE · PALEO

This hash recipe combines some of my favorite things: eggs and potatoes, and breakfast in general. Making potato noodles has made a world of a difference in my life because it cuts down significantly on cook time. You can make a big batch of this delicious breakfast and save the leftovers for the next day (if you even have leftovers!).

Serves 2
Prep time: 5 minutes
Cook time: 25 minutes
Blade: C

6 to 8 ounces bacon or pancetta, diced

1 onion, spiralized

1 large potato, spiralized

½ red or green bell pepper, spiralized

4 large eggs

Salt

Freshly ground black pepper

1. In a large nonstick skillet over medium heat, cook the diced bacon for about 5 minutes, until it begins to brown and release some cooking fat.

2. Add the onion and cook for 2 to 3 minutes, or until softened slightly. Add the potato and bell pepper noodles and cook for 10 to 12 minutes more, stirring occasionally, until fork-tender.

3. While the potatoes are cooking, in a small bowl, whisk the eggs. (You can skip this step if you want to fry the eggs instead of scrambling them.) Add the eggs to the skillet and scramble until firm, 3 to 4 minutes, incorporating the eggs into the spiralized veggies. (If frying the eggs, remove the potato hash from the pan, fry the eggs, then serve over the hash.)

4. Season with salt and pepper and serve immediately.

TIP: Make this a vegetarian dish by omitting the bacon or pancetta and using 2 tablespoons of olive oil or butter instead of the fat from the meat.

PER SERVING Calories: 704; Saturated Fat: 18g; Total Fat: 55g; Protein: 29g; Total Carbs: 24g; Fiber: 4g; Sodium: 968mg

Sweet Potato Noodle Breakfast Bowls

ONE POT • PALEO

If you get into the habit of pre-spiralizing (and even sautéing) some veggies every week, you'll be ready with these sweet potato noodle breakfast bowls with little to no planning needed—just fill a bowl with the noodles and top with your favorite veggies, some eggs, maybe bacon or sausage, and a sprinkle of cheese or hot sauce. In just a few minutes, you'll have a breakfast that's quick, easy, filling, and delicious.

Serves 2
Prep time: 5 minutes
Cook time: 15 minutes
Blade: C

2 tablespoons grass-fed butter, plus more for cooking the eggs

½ onion, spiralized or diced

1 garlic clove, minced

2 large sweet potatoes, peeled and spiralized

Salt

Freshly ground black pepper

4 large eggs

1 cup fresh spinach

2 to 4 cooked bacon slices, chopped

½ cup shredded Cheddar cheese

1. In a large nonstick skillet over medium heat, melt the butter. Add the onion and garlic and cook for about 3 minutes, stirring frequently.

2. Add the sweet potato noodles, and sauté for another 5 to 7 minutes, or until cooked through. Season with salt and pepper, and remove from the heat. Divide the sweet potato noodles between two bowls and keep warm.

3. Return the pan to the heat and add a little more butter. Cook the eggs to your liking: If you want them scrambled, whisk them in a bowl and cook over medium heat, stirring occasionally, for 4 to 5 minutes or until set. You can also fry them (I like mine over-medium) for 2 to 3 minutes, then flip carefully to cook the other side for about a minute.

4. Assemble the breakfast bowls by layering the spinach, chopped bacon, eggs, and Cheddar cheese over the sweet potato noodles. Serve immediately.

TIP: Make this a keto recipe by using zucchini or summer squash noodles instead of sweet potatoes and topping each bowl with ½ a sliced avocado. If you want to wilt your spinach slightly, toss it in with the sweet potato noodles about a minute before you remove them from the heat.

PER SERVING Calories: 693; Saturated Fat: 22g; Total Fat: 47g; Protein: 37g; Total Carbs: 32g; Fiber: 5g; Sodium: 1437mg

Spiralized Veggie Egg Muffins

5-INGREDIENT · DAIRY-FREE · PALEO · VEGETARIAN

These egg muffins are the ultimate meal-prep recipe—you can make a batch on Sunday night and have them for breakfast for the rest of the week. I make them when I'm already preparing a meal, so when everything is done I have the meal we're about to enjoy plus a batch of egg muffins for future breakfasts and snacking.

Makes 12 muffins
Prep time: 5 minutes
Cook time: 25 minutes
Blade: D

1 tablespoon olive oil, plus more for greasing

1 red onion, spiralized

1 green bell pepper, spiralized

½ zucchini, spiralized

1 garlic clove, minced

9 large eggs, beaten

1. Preheat the oven to 350°F.

2. In a large skillet over medium-high heat, heat the olive oil. Sauté the onion, bell pepper, and zucchini noodles with the garlic for about 2 to 3 minutes, or until softened. Remove from the heat.

3. Lightly grease a muffin tin with olive oil.

4. Pour the eggs into each muffin cup, and divide the sautéed veggie mixture evenly among them.

5. Bake for 22 minutes, or until the eggs are firm, and serve.

TIP: To make this a keto-friendly recipe, add ½ cup of shredded cheese to the egg mixture and top each muffin with a slice of avocado before serving.

PER SERVING Calories: 70; Saturated Fat: 1g; Total Fat: 5g; Protein: 5g; Total Carbs: 2g; Fiber: 0g; Sodium: 54mg

Breakfast Frittata with Spiralized Potato Crust

ONE POT • DAIRY-FREE • PALEO

Breakfast frittatas are my go-to when I have a bunch of ingredients in my refrigerator and no real plans for them—I throw them in a skillet with some butter or olive oil and add eggs, maybe some cheese, and the result is always a delicious breakfast that people love. This time I added some spiralized potato to give it a nice crust, and I don't know if I'll ever make it differently! This recipe takes a little longer than 30 minutes, but you'll be glad you took the extra time to make this crowd-pleaser.

Serves 4
Prep time: 5 minutes
Cook time: 40 minutes
Blade: D

3 tablespoons olive oil

¼ onion, chopped

1 garlic clove, minced

1 large white potato, spiralized

5 ounces breakfast sausage, casings removed

Salt

Freshly ground black pepper

6 large eggs, beaten

2 tablespoons sliced scallion, for garnish

1. Preheat the oven to 375°F.

2. In a large oven-safe skillet over medium heat, heat the olive oil. Sauté the onion and garlic until the onion is translucent, 5 to 7 minutes. Add the potato noodles and cook for 4 to 5 minutes until tender.

3. Add the sausage to the pan and cook until no more pink remains, about 6 minutes, breaking it up as you stir. Season with salt and pepper. Stir all the contents of the pan together well to make sure everything is combined evenly, then pour the eggs over the potato mixture and transfer the pan to the oven.

4. Bake for 15 to 20 minutes, or until the eggs are set. Cut into wedges and serve hot, garnished with a sprinkle of scallions.

TIP: Skip the potato crust to make this a keto-friendly recipe.

PER SERVING Calories: 316; Saturated Fat: 6g; Total Fat: 25g; Protein: 16g; Total Carbs: 9g; Fiber: 2g; Sodium: 325mg

Southwestern Steak Salad, *page 43*

Soups, Salads & Sandwiches

Soups and salads are some of the easiest places to incorporate veggie noodles into your diet. Sandwiches, not so much, but this chapter is full of great lunch and dinner recipes that cover all three categories. You'll find new ideas and old favorites, from steaming bowls of ramen and classics like chicken noodle soup to fast no-cook salads and some fun sandwich ideas. I hope these next pages inspire you to get creative with your lunch game.

Chicken Zoodle Soup

ONE POT • DAIRY-FREE • PALEO

This is a 30-minutes-or-less spin on my favorite chicken soup recipe, which I like to make from scratch when I have time, but let's face it—bone broth takes almost a full day to make, and sometimes we just don't have time for that. Garlic, celery, onion, and carrots come together in olive oil to flavor store-bought chicken broth and make this soup just as delicious, but way quicker from stove to table.

Serves 4 to 6
Prep time: 5 minutes
Cook time: 20 minutes
Blade: B

1 tablespoon olive oil

1½ onions, spiralized

2 garlic cloves, minced

3 carrots, spiralized

½ head celery, spiralized (this will mostly just chop it for you; you won't end up with noodles but that's okay)

Salt

Freshly ground black pepper

2 (32-ounce) cartons chicken broth

8 to 10 ounces diced chicken breast or thigh

2 medium zucchini, spiralized

1. In a large stockpot over medium heat, heat the olive oil. Sauté the onions, garlic, carrots, and celery for 2 to 3 minutes, stirring occasionally, until the veggies have softened slightly. Season with salt and pepper.

2. Pour the chicken broth into the pot and bring to a low boil. Add the chicken and simmer until cooked through, 5 to 7 minutes. Continue to simmer for 10 minutes more, adding the zucchini noodles to the pot 1 to 2 minutes before you're ready to serve (or even after you turn off the heat—they only need to soften in the hot soup).

3. Ladle into bowls and serve.

TIP: Make this a vegetarian soup by leaving out the chicken and using vegetable broth instead.

PER SERVING Calories: 256; Saturated Fat: 1g; Total Fat: 8g; Protein: 28g; Total Carbs: 17g; Fiber: 5g; Sodium: 1732mg

Carrot Noodle Ramen

DAIRY-FREE • PALEO

I absolutely love ramen (and most soups), and I used to make this recipe with zucchini noodles, but lately I've found that I like it so much more with carrot noodles. They hold up better to the broth and add a bit of a crunch that I really enjoy. Plus, thinly sliced carrots are just great with almost any Asian cuisine, so it's a win-win when it comes to both flavor and texture.

Serves 4
Prep time: 10 minutes
Cook time: 20 minutes
Blade: D

6 to 8 cups chicken or beef broth

1½ bunches scallions, plus more for optional garnish

2 ounces peeled fresh ginger, thinly sliced (about ½ cup)

4 garlic cloves, minced

Toppings (optional): chopped softboiled eggs, kimchi, sliced jalapeños, chopped scallion, chopped fresh cilantro

5 tablespoons coconut aminos (or gluten-free soy sauce)

2 tablespoons sake (omit if strict Paleo)

1½ tablespoons sesame oil

1 pound cooked pork tenderloin, thinly sliced

1 pound spiralized carrots

1. In a large stockpot over medium-high heat, heat the broth. Add the scallions, ginger, and garlic. Bring to a boil, then lower the heat and simmer for 10 to 15 minutes.

2. Prepare the toppings while the broth simmers: Soft boil the eggs (cook in boiling water for about 6 minutes), and slice the jalapeños, scallions, and/or cilantro.

3. Add the coconut aminos, sake (if using), and sesame oil to the broth. Add the sliced pork and carrot noodles, and continue to simmer for 5 to 7 minutes.

4. Ladle into bowls, add toppings of your choice, and serve hot.

TIP: Make vegetarian ramen by omitting the pork and using vegetable broth instead. Skip the softboiled eggs, too, for a vegan dish.

PER SERVING Calories: 370; Saturated Fat: 3g; Total Fat: 12g; Protein: 41g; Total Carbs: 21g; Fiber: 4g; Sodium: 1696mg

Tortilla Soup with Sweet Potato Noodles

My family is absolutely obsessed with tortilla soup—there's a restaurant in the Bay Area that makes our favorite, and we always stop and have it for lunch or dinner whenever we're together. I decided to make a Paleo version with sweet potato noodles instead of tortilla strips to keep it grain-free. The spicy broth and creamy avocado with fresh lime is such a delicious combination that I don't even miss the chips!

Serves 4
Prep time: 5 minutes
Cook time: 20 minutes
Blade: B

2 tablespoons olive oil

1 onion, diced or spiralized and roughly chopped

4 garlic cloves, minced

2 large sweet potatoes, peeled and spiralized

6 cups chicken broth

1 (28-ounce) can crushed tomatoes (no sugar added)

1 tablespoon paprika

2 teaspoons ground cumin

1 teaspoon chili powder

¼ teaspoon cayenne pepper

2 bay leaves

Salt

Freshly ground black pepper

1 pound boneless chicken breast, diced

1 cup shredded Cheddar cheese

1 or 2 avocados, quartered or diced

¼ cup chopped fresh cilantro, for garnish

Lime wedges, for serving

1. In a large stockpot over medium heat, heat the olive oil. Sauté the onion and garlic for 2 to 3 minutes, or until the garlic is fragrant and the onion is softened slightly, then add the sweet potato noodles. Cook for 5 to 7 minutes, stirring occasionally, then remove the noodles from the heat and set aside in a large bowl.

2. Return the pot to the heat, and add the chicken broth, tomatoes, paprika, cumin, chili powder, cayenne, and bay leaves. Season with salt and pepper. Bring to a boil, and reduce the heat to a simmer. If desired, use an immersion blender to purée the broth until smooth (be sure to remove the bay leaves first).

3. Add the chicken and continue to simmer until cooked through, 3 to 5 minutes. Remove the bay leaves if you haven't already.

4. Ladle the soup into bowls and top with the reserved sweet potato noodles, Cheddar, and avocado. Garnish with a generous sprinkle of cilantro and a wedge of lime and serve.

TIP: Make this soup vegetarian by using diced tofu and vegetable broth instead of the chicken and chicken broth (or omit the protein entirely).

PER SERVING Calories: 747; Saturated Fat: 13g; Total Fat: 42g; Protein: 49g; Total Carbs: 47g; Fiber: 18g; Sodium: 2292mg

Thai Noodle Soup

ONE POT • VEGAN

This veggie-packed noodle soup is so comforting on a chilly afternoon. I love Asian flavors, so I often make quick Thai-inspired dishes like this one. All the veggies (except for the mushrooms) are spiralized to add even more noodles, but also to cut down on prep time as much as possible so you can get to enjoying this warm, comforting, healthy meal.

Serves 4
Prep time: 10 minutes
Cook time: 20 minutes
Blade: C

1 tablespoon olive oil

2 carrots, spiralized

1 onion, spiralized

2 garlic cloves, minced

1 tablespoon minced
fresh ginger

5 to 6 ounces shiitake
mushrooms, stemmed and
thinly sliced

Salt

Freshly ground black pepper

4 to 6 cups vegetable broth

2 tablespoons gluten-free
soy sauce

Juice of 1 lime, plus lime
wedges for serving

1 large zucchini, spiralized

½ thinly sliced jalapeño,
pepper stemmed and seeded

¼ cup chopped fresh
cilantro, for garnish

1. In a large stockpot over medium heat, heat the olive oil. Sauté the carrot noodles, onion, garlic, and ginger for 3 minutes.

2. Add the mushrooms and stir well to combine. Season with salt and pepper.

3. Pour the vegetable broth into the pot and bring to a low simmer. Cook for 10 minutes, then add the soy sauce and lime juice.

4. Add the zucchini noodles and jalapeño and cook for 2 to 3 minutes more until the noodles are tender.

5. Ladle into serving bowls and serve hot, garnished with cilantro and a wedge of lime.

TIP: If you eat meat, make this soup Paleo (and add some more protein) by using beef broth and adding about 1 pound of thinly sliced steak to the pot with the mushrooms. If strict Paleo, use coconut aminos instead of soy sauce.

PER SERVING Calories: 149; Saturated Fat: 1g; Total Fat: 6g; Protein: 11g; Total Carbs: 15g; Fiber: 4g; Sodium: 1686mg

Spiralized "Tortellini" Sausage Soup

ONE POT · DAIRY-FREE · PALEO

This spicy sausage soup uses spiralized summer squash noodles instead of traditional tortellini—it's a Paleo recipe, so there's no cheese, but the ribbon noodles give it that tortellini vibe that's always fun in a soup like this. Beef broth, spicy sausage, and a little red wine make this an incredibly satisfying meal that's perfect for a chilly winter's night.

Serves 4
Prep time: 5 minutes
Cook time: 25 minutes
Blade: A

1 tablespoon olive oil

1 onion, spiralized on blade D or diced

1 or 2 garlic cloves, minced

1 pound spicy Italian sausage, casings removed

4 cups beef broth

1 (6-ounce) can tomato paste

½ cup red wine (optional if strict Paleo)

¼ teaspoon dried oregano

Salt

Freshly ground black pepper

3 or 4 medium summer squash, spiralized and trimmed into short pieces

¼ cup chopped fresh basil, for garnish

1. In a large stockpot over medium heat, heat the olive oil. Sauté the onion and garlic for 3 minutes. Add the sausage and brown for 4 to 5 minutes, breaking it up with a wooden spoon.

2. Add the beef broth and tomato paste, stirring well to combine. Add the wine and oregano. Season with salt and pepper and bring to a low simmer for 10 to 15 minutes, adding the summer squash noodles about 3 minutes before you're ready to serve.

3. Ladle into serving bowls and top with fresh basil. Enjoy immediately.

TIP: If you tolerate dairy, serve this soup with some freshly grated Parmesan cheese.

PER SERVING Calories: 564; Saturated Fat: 14g; Total Fat: 41g; Protein: 26g; Total Carbs: 20g; Fiber: 5g; Sodium: 1692mg

Pasta e Fagioli

ONE POT • VEGETARIAN

"Pasta e fagioli" means "pasta and beans" in Italian, and this soup is a filling and flavorful vegetarian dish that can be made in 30 minutes or less if you use store-bought broth and canned beans. I've substituted the macaroni or small-shell pasta you'll normally find in this soup with spiralized and chopped butternut squash noodles. It's even better with a little extra Parmesan cheese on top.

Serves 4
Prep time: 5 minutes
Cook time: 25 minutes
Blade: B

1 tablespoon olive oil

1 onion, diced or spiralized

1 garlic clove, minced

1 butternut squash, spiralized and chopped into elbow macaroni shape

4 cups vegetable broth

1 (28-ounce) can crushed tomatoes (no sugar added)

¼ teaspoon red pepper flakes

Salt

Freshly ground black pepper

1 (15-ounce) can pinto beans, rinsed and drained

½ cup grated Parmesan cheese, for serving

2 tablespoons chopped fresh parsley, for garnish

1. In a large stockpot over medium heat, heat the olive oil and sauté the onion and garlic for 2 to 3 minutes, or until the garlic is fragrant and the onion is softened slightly. Add the butternut squash "pasta" and continue to sauté for another 3 to 4 minutes.

2. Add the vegetable broth and tomatoes, and bring to a low boil. Add the red pepper flakes, and season with salt and pepper. Simmer for 10 minutes.

3. Add the beans to the soup, and stir gently to combine. Continue to cook until the beans are heated through, 5 to 10 minutes.

4. Ladle into bowls and top with Parmesan cheese. Serve hot, garnished with chopped parsley.

TIP: Make this soup Paleo by swapping the beans for about a pound of Italian sausage and eliminating the Parmesan cheese. See the Spiralized "Tortellini" Sausage Soup recipe for cooking instructions (page 36).

PER SERVING Calories: 423; Saturated Fat: 3g; Total Fat: 9g; Protein: 24g; Total Carbs: 67g; Fiber: 19g; Sodium: 1326mg

Spiralized Cucumber Salad

NO COOK • PALEO • VEGAN

The combination of cucumbers, tomatoes, and red onion always makes me feel like I'm going to a cookout. This recipe is perfect for your next summer party. I spiralize the cucumbers and red onion for two different kinds of noodle, then add sliced cherry tomatoes and a quick balsamic vinaigrette. Top it with a handful of fresh basil for even more summer goodness.

Serves 2 to 4
Prep time: 10 minutes
Blade: A

2 or 3 cucumbers, spiralized

¼ red onion, spiralized with blade B or C or thinly sliced

1 cup cherry tomatoes, halved

½ cup olive oil

½ cup balsamic vinegar

1 tablespoon Dijon mustard

Salt

Freshly ground black pepper

2 to 3 tablespoons chopped fresh basil, for garnish

1. In a large bowl, combine the cucumber noodles, onion, and cherry tomatoes.

2. In a small bowl, whisk the olive oil, balsamic vinegar, and Dijon mustard. Season with salt and pepper.

3. Pour the dressing over the salad and toss to combine. Garnish with the basil and serve immediately.

TIP: To make this salad keto instead of vegan, add some diced mozzarella for extra fat.

PER SERVING Calories: 540; Saturated Fat: 7g; Total Fat: 51g; Protein: 4g; Total Carbs: 22g; Fiber: 4g; Sodium: 183mg

Veggie Noodle Salad

NO COOK • ONE POT • DAIRY-FREE • PALEO • VEGETARIAN

This salad is a quick and easy way to put together a delicious side dish that's packed with colorful vegetables. I especially enjoy the flavor of the sweet apple cider dressing with the crisp, raw veggie noodles. Switching up the blades that I use to spiralize the veggies gives this dish a variety of textures, and giving them a quick trim makes it easy to eat.

Serves 2
Prep time: 10 minutes
Blade: A, B, and D

2 tablespoons olive oil

2 tablespoons honey

1 tablespoon apple cider vinegar

1 tablespoon Dijon mustard

¼ teaspoon red pepper flakes

Salt

Freshly ground black pepper

1 large zucchini, spiralized

2 or 3 carrots, spiralized

1 red bell pepper, spiralized

1. In a large bowl, combine the olive oil, honey, apple cider vinegar, Dijon mustard, and red pepper flakes. Season with salt and pepper.

2. Add the zucchini, carrot, and bell pepper noodles and toss gently to combine.

3. Serve immediately.

TIP: Use agave nectar instead of honey for a vegan version of this salad.

PER SERVING Calories: 270; Saturated Fat: 2g; Total Fat: 15g; Protein: 3g; Total Carbs: 36g; Fiber: 5g; Sodium: 242mg

Spiralized Waldorf Salad

DAIRY-FREE • PALEO • VEGETARIAN

There are lots of variations on the classic Waldorf salad, which is usually a mayonnaise-based dish with apples, grapes, and walnuts served over lettuce. You can use yogurt if you aren't into mayonnaise (and maybe add a tablespoon of honey), but I'm a huge fan of mayo so this recipe is a bit more on the traditional side, with the exception of spiralizing the apples instead of dicing them.

Serves 2 to 4
Prep time: 10 minutes
Cook time: 5 minutes
Blade: C

¼ cup mayonnaise

1 tablespoon freshly squeezed lemon juice

2 or 3 apples, cored and spiralized

1 head of celery, spiralized (this will just chop it but saves you prep time)

1 cup seedless red grapes, halved

Salt

Freshly ground black pepper

1 cup walnuts

1 head romaine lettuce

1. In a large bowl, combine the mayonnaise and lemon juice. Add the apple noodles, celery, and grapes, stirring gently to combine. Season with salt and pepper.

2. In a small skillet over low heat, heat the walnuts, gently shaking the pan to prevent any burnt spots. Cook until lightly toasted and fragrant, about 4 minutes, keeping a close eye to be sure they don't burn and shaking the skillet frequently. Give the walnuts a rough chop and add them to the bowl with the fruit. Toss to combine.

3. Divide the lettuce among serving bowls and top with the apple-celery-grape-walnut mixture. Serve immediately.

TIP: If not vegetarian, make this more of a main dish by adding about ½ pound of diced or shredded cooked chicken breast to the bowl with the fruit and celery, along with a little extra mayonnaise, if desired.

PER SERVING Calories: 708; Saturated Fat: 5g; Total Fat: 44g; Protein: 11g; Total Carbs: 82g; Fiber: 14g; Sodium: 370mg

Spiralized Niçoise Salad

DAIRY-FREE • PALEO

There's a little French café in Sonoma that my husband and I always stop at after we visit our favorite winery, where I once had the best Niçoise salad ever. Instead of just hoping to see it on the menu again every time we pass through, I started making my own at home. I couldn't resist using my spiralizer to prepare the potato so now I've made the best Niçoise salad ever even better.

Serves 1 or 2
Prep time: 10 minutes
Cook time: 10 minutes
Blade: C

FOR THE SALAD

1 large potato, spiralized

3 to 4 ounces green beans

1 large head
romaine, chopped

¼ cup black olives

4 radishes, trimmed and quartered

1 hardboiled egg (cooked in boiling water for about 10 minutes), quartered

1 Roma tomato, quartered

1 (12-ounce) can tuna

FOR THE VINAIGRETTE

½ shallot, minced

1 tablespoon Dijon mustard

¼ cup white wine vinegar

½ cup olive oil

Salt

Freshly ground black pepper

TO MAKE THE SALAD

1. Bring a large stockpot of water to a boil. Cook the potato noodles for 3 to 4 minutes, or until fork-tender, then remove them from the pot with a slotted spoon or strainer and blanch in a large bowl of cold water. Drain and set aside.

2. In the same boiling water, cook the green beans for 5 minutes until crisp-tender. Remove them from the pot with a slotted spoon or strainer and blanch in cold water. Drain and set aside.

3. Place the lettuce in a large bowl. Arrange the potato noodles, green beans, olives, radishes, hardboiled egg, and tomato over the lettuce. Add the tuna.

TO MAKE THE VINAIGRETTE

In a small bowl, whisk the shallot, Dijon mustard, and white wine vinegar. Continue to whisk as you slowly pour in the olive oil. Season with salt and pepper and pour over the salad, tossing gently to combine. Serve immediately.

TIP: Make this salad keto by omitting the potato noodles and adding a quartered avocado. Make the potato a sweet potato if strict Paleo.

PER SERVING Calories: 1512; Saturated Fat: 16g; Total Fat: 113g; Protein: 37g; Total Carbs: 108g; Fiber: 16g; Sodium: 957mg

Asian Chicken Salad

ONE POT • DAIRY-FREE

I can never resist a Chinese-style chicken salad like this one—the crunchy cabbage and carrots combined with chicken and sesame vinaigrette are such a great combination with sweet edamame and zesty scallions. This hearty salad is substantial enough to serve as a main meal.

Serves 4
Prep time: 15 minutes
Blade: A and D

¼ cup rice vinegar

2 tablespoons sesame oil

1 teaspoon gluten-free soy sauce

1 teaspoon minced fresh ginger

1 garlic clove, minced

1 pound cooked chicken breast, diced or sliced

2 large heads romaine lettuce, chopped

1 small head red cabbage, spiralized (blade A)

2 medium carrots, spiralized (blade D)

¼ cup shelled edamame

¼ cup sliced almonds

1 or 2 scallions, sliced, for garnish

1. In a large bowl, whisk the rice vinegar, sesame oil, soy sauce, ginger, and garlic until smooth.

2. Add the chicken, lettuce, cabbage, carrot noodles, edamame, and almonds. Toss gently to combine, and transfer to serving bowls. Top with the scallions and serve.

TIP: Make this salad Paleo by omitting the edamame and replacing the soy sauce with coconut aminos and adding some canned mandarin oranges (if desired).

PER SERVING Calories: 428; Saturated Fat: 3g; Total Fat: 16g; Protein: 48g; Total Carbs: 19g; Fiber: 11g; Sodium: 219mg

Southwestern Steak Salad

KETO

This Southwestern steak salad takes the taco salad up a notch by using medium-rare seared steak instead of ground beef. Cherry tomatoes, Cheddar, and creamy avocado round out the dish perfectly, and the addition of cucumber and carrot noodles not only cuts down on the time chopping vegetables, it also adds fun new textures to the salad. Get this on the table quickly by spiralizing and slicing your veggies while the steak is resting.

Serves 2 to 4
Prep time: 10 minutes
Cook time: 20 minutes
Blade: D

1 pound steak
(such as flank steak)

1 tablespoon olive oil

Salt

Freshly ground black pepper

1 tablespoon grass-fed butter

2 or 3 heads romaine
lettuce, chopped

¾ cup sliced cherry tomatoes

¼ to ½ cup ranch dressing
(or your favorite sugar-free
dressing)

½ cup shredded
Cheddar cheese

2 carrots, spiralized

1 cucumber, spiralized

1 avocado, quartered
and sliced

¼ cup chopped fresh
cilantro, for garnish

1. Drizzle the steak with the olive oil, then season with salt and pepper. Heat a grill or cast iron skillet to medium-high heat, then cook the steak for 7 to 8 minutes per side for medium-rare, or more or less according to your preference. Remove from the heat, top with the butter, and allow to rest for 10 minutes before slicing.

2. In a large bowl, toss the chopped lettuce with the tomatoes, ranch dressing (or dressing of your choice), and Cheddar. Gently mix in the carrot and cucumber noodles and the avocado, and season with salt and pepper.

3. Transfer to two large bowls for serving. Top with the sliced steak, garnish with the cilantro, and enjoy immediately.

TIP: Make this salad vegetarian instead of keto by skipping the steak and adding a can of black beans and a can of corn instead.

PER SERVING Calories: 1024; Saturated Fat: 26g; Total Fat: 67g; Protein: 75g;
Total Carbs: 33g; Fiber: 11g; Sodium: 888mg

Ham and Cheese on Sweet Potato Noodle Buns

5-INGREDIENT

A ham and cheese sandwich might be one of the simplest lunches in the world, but when you heat it up and serve it on a sweet potato noodle bun, it's a little more interesting. It's a cinch to make these sweet potato noodle buns and top them with your favorite sandwich ingredients for easy lunches. Smear a little Dijon mustard on this sandwich if you're feeling extra fancy.

Serves 2
Prep time: 10 minutes
Cook time: 20 minutes
Blade: D

FOR THE SWEET POTATO NOODLE BUNS

1 large sweet potato, spiralized

3 tablespoons olive oil, divided

1 large egg, whisked

Salt

Freshly ground black pepper

FOR THE SANDWICHES

4 Cheddar or provolone cheese slices

8 ounces sliced ham

TO MAKE THE SWEET POTATO NOODLE BUNS

1. In a large nonstick skillet over medium-high heat, sauté the sweet potato noodles in 1½ tablespoons of olive oil for 4 to 5 minutes until softened. Transfer to a medium bowl and cool slightly. Toss with the egg, and season with salt and pepper. Transfer the mixture to four ramekins or round cookie cutters (about 5-inch diameter), pressing down slightly to pack them in. Pop them into the refrigerator for a few minutes to set.

2. Wipe the skillet clean and return it to medium-high heat with the remaining 1½ tablespoons of olive oil. Carefully remove the noodle cakes from the ramekins. Fry the noodle cakes for 3 to 4 minutes per side, or until browned and crispy.

TO MAKE THE SANDWICHES

Reduce the heat to low and add a slice of cheese to each "bun." Heat until the cheese is melted. Top one side with ham and carefully place two buns together, cheese-side in, to create a sandwich. Serve immediately.

TIP: Add a fried or scrambled egg to each sandwich for some additional protein or to make it more of a brunch dish.

PER SERVING Calories: 682; Saturated Fat: 19g; Total Fat: 52g; Protein: 37g; Total Carbs: 18g; Fiber: 3g; Sodium: 1970mg

Buffalo Chicken Sandwiches on Carrot Noodle Buns

5-INGREDIENT • PALEO

We are huge Buffalo chicken fans in my family, and I'm always looking for new, healthy ways to incorporate the flavor of Buffalo sauce into our meals. My husband grew up eating the most delicious Buffalo chicken cheesesteaks, and while we haven't recreated the recipe 100 percent yet, this Paleo version on carrot noodle buns is darn close.

Serves 2
Prep time: 10 minutes
Cook time: 15 minutes
Blade: D

FOR THE CARROT NOODLE BUNS

4 or 5 carrots, spiralized

3 tablespoons olive oil, divided

1 large egg, beaten

Salt

Freshly ground black pepper

FOR THE SANDWICHES

4 tablespoons (½ stick) grass-fed butter, melted

¼ cup Frank's hot sauce

2 large chicken breasts, cooked and shredded

TO MAKE THE CARROT NOODLE BUNS

1. In a large nonstick skillet over medium-high heat, sauté the carrot noodles in 1½ tablespoons of olive oil for 4 to 5 minutes, or until softened. Transfer to a medium bowl, cool slightly, and toss with the egg. Transfer to four ramekins or round cookie cutters (about 5-inch diameter), pressing down slightly to pack them in. Pop them into the refrigerator for a few minutes to set.

2. Remove the carrot noodle cakes from the ramekins, wipe the skillet clean, and fry the cakes in the remaining 1½ tablespoons of olive oil over medium-high heat for 3 to 4 minutes per side, or until browned and crispy.

TO MAKE THE SANDWICHES

1. While the carrot noodle cakes are chilling, in a small bowl, mix the butter and hot sauce together. In a large bowl, pour the sauce over the chicken and toss well to combine. If the chicken isn't saucy enough for you, make more, using a 1:1 ratio of butter to hot sauce.

2. Transfer two carrot noodle cakes to plates, and divide the chicken mixture equally between them. Top with the remaining cakes and serve immediately.

TIP: The carrot noodle buns remind me of the carrots tradition-ally served with Buffalo chicken, but you can use sweet potato or white potato noodle buns if carrots aren't your thing.

PER SERVING Calories: 658; Saturated Fat: 20g; Total Fat: 46g; Protein: 45g; Total Carbs: 15g; Fiber: 4g; Sodium: 559mg

Club Sandwich on Cauliflower Bread

KETO

My favorite sandwich for lunch has to be a club—I love turkey, but even more so when it's combined with ham, bacon, and some crisp lettuce and juicy tomato. These sandwiches use the same bread as the bacon, egg, and cheese sandwiches you'll find in the breakfast chapter (page 23). It's great how versatile this bread recipe can be! I love having it in the refrigerator so I can quickly make a sandwich like this one for lunch when I'm working from home (or you can wrap it up and take it with you).

Serves 2
Prep time: 10 minutes
Cook time: 20 minutes

FOR THE CAULIFLOWER BREAD

1 head cauliflower

3 large eggs

1 shallot, minced

1 teaspoon dried oregano

1 teaspoon chopped
fresh chives

1 teaspoon chopped
fresh parsley

3 garlic cloves, chopped

1 teaspoon salt

Freshly ground black pepper

FOR THE SANDWICHES

2 tablespoons mayonnaise

4 ounces sliced turkey

4 ounces sliced ham

2 Cheddar or Havarti
cheese slices

2 romaine lettuce leaves

2 tomato slices

4 cooked bacon slices

TO MAKE THE CAULIFLOWER BREAD

1. Preheat the oven to 350°F.

2. In a food processor, pulse the cauliflower until the pieces resemble grains of rice. Transfer to a microwave-safe bowl. Cook on high in the microwave for 2 minutes. Allow to cool for a few minutes, then twist in a thin cloth or cheesecloth to remove any water (not a lot will come out, but the little that's there needs to be removed). If you don't have a food processor, use a box grater to shred the cauliflower.

3. Transfer the cauliflower to a medium bowl. In a smaller bowl, whisk the eggs with the shallot, oregano, chives, parsley, garlic, salt, and a few twists of pepper. Pour the mixture over the cauliflower and stir together until well incorporated.

4. Line a large baking sheet with parchment paper or aluminum foil. Scoop on the cauliflower mixture in four equal parts, then spread them out until each is about a ¼ inch thick, with a little room in between. Bake for 10 minutes, then flip and bake for another 7 minutes. Remove from the oven and allow to cool slightly.

TO MAKE THE SANDWICHES

Add a tablespoon of mayonnaise to one side of two pieces of cauliflower bread, then layer with turkey, ham, cheese, lettuce, tomato, and bacon. Top with another piece of cauliflower bread and serve.

TIP: Make these Paleo and dairy-free by omitting the cheese.

PER SERVING Calories: 658; Saturated Fat: 12g; Total Fat: 32g; Protein: 60g; Total Carbs: 18g; Fiber: 5g; Sodium: 3248mg

Grilled Cheese Sandwiches on Cauliflower Bread

KETO • VEGETARIAN

A grilled cheese might be one of my all-time favorite sandwiches. Sometimes I'll have one on gluten-free bread, but it's so nice to stay grain-free with these delicious cheesy cauliflower sandwiches. I add cheese to both the bread and the sandwich to make these extra cheesy. They're delicious on their own or with tomato soup and/or a salad. And you can always add avocado, bacon, or any other fun extras you like!

Serves 2
Prep time: 10 minutes
Cook time: 20 minutes

FOR THE CAULIFLOWER BREAD

1 head cauliflower

3 large eggs

¼ cup shredded Parmesan or Cheddar cheese

1 shallot, minced

1 teaspoon dried oregano

1 teaspoon chopped fresh chives

1 teaspoon chopped fresh parsley

3 garlic cloves, chopped

1 teaspoon salt

Freshly ground black pepper

FOR THE SANDWICHES

4 slices your favorite cheese (I almost always use Cheddar)

TO MAKE THE CAULIFLOWER BREAD

1. Preheat the oven to 350°F.

2. In a food processor, pulse the cauliflower until the pieces resemble grains of rice. Transfer to a microwave-safe bowl. Cook on high in the microwave for 2 minutes. Allow to cool for a few minutes, then twist in a thin cloth or cheesecloth to remove any water (not a lot will come out, but the little that's there needs to be removed). If you don't have a food processor, use a box grater to shred the cauliflower.

3. Transfer the cauliflower to a medium bowl. In a smaller bowl, whisk the eggs together with the shredded cheese, shallot, oregano, chives, parsley, garlic, salt, and a few twists of pepper. Pour the mixture over the cauliflower and stir together until well incorporated.

4. Line a large baking sheet with parchment paper or aluminum foil. Scoop on the cauliflower mixture in four equal parts, then spread them out until they're about a ¼ inch thick, with a little room in between. Bake for 10 minutes, then flip and bake for another 7 minutes. Remove from the oven and allow to cool slightly.

TO MAKE THE SANDWICHES

Add a slice of cheese to each piece of cauliflower bread and pop back in the oven until melted. Put them together to make sandwiches and serve immediately.

TIP: Eliminate the extra cheese in the cauliflower bread and use dairy-free cheese slices for nondairy sandwiches.

PER SERVING Calories: 425; Saturated Fat: 16g; Total Fat: 29g; Protein: 31g; Total Carbs: 12g; Fiber: 4g; Sodium: 1789mg

Spiralized Sweet Potato Chips, *page 53*

Snacks & Sides

When you're trying to eat healthier, finding good snacks and side dishes can be challenging, especially since so many of us tend to snack on carb-loaded foods like chips and crackers. This chapter is full of healthy side dishes and easy snacks that you can take with you on the go—mostly fruit-and-veggie-loaded salads as well as spiralized versions of pasta salads, but you'll also find some chips and hot side dishes that are a perfect way to round out your spiralized meals.

Spiralized Quick Pickles

5-INGREDIENT • DAIRY-FREE • PALEO • VEGETARIAN

I love having these pickles in my refrigerator for sandwiches or a little snack on their own. They don't keep as long as regular pickles you'd buy at the store, which tend to be full of preservatives, but I never find that to be a problem because we eat them so fast! My husband doesn't even like pickles that much but can't resist these homemade ones, especially on top of a homemade burger.

Serves 4
Prep time: 10 minutes
Cook time: 10 minutes
Blade: A

½ cup red wine vinegar

½ cup water

¼ cup honey

1 tablespoon black peppercorns

1 tablespoon mustard seeds

2 large cucumbers, spiralized

1. In a small saucepan over high heat, combine the vinegar, water, honey, peppercorns, and mustard seeds. Bring to a boil.

2. While the brine boils, pack the cucumber noodles into clean jars. Remove the brine from the heat and carefully pour it over the cucumbers. Allow the pickles to come to room temperature, then cover and refrigerate for at least 2 hours or up to 10 days.

TIP: Make this a vegan recipe by skipping the honey. Use sugar or a little agave nectar instead. Be sure to taste the brine when making substitutions to make sure it isn't too sweet.

PER SERVING Calories: 93; Saturated Fat: 0g; Total Fat: 0g; Protein: 1g; Total Carbs: 23g; Fiber: 1g; Sodium: 5mg

Baked Cinnamon Apple Chips

5-INGREDIENT • ONE POT • PALEO • VEGETARIAN

When fall rolls around every year I get so excited to bake apples and pumpkins and all kinds of festive, autumn-inspired treats. These quick-baked apple chips are perfect as a snack or treat, and this recipe comes in handy if you're like us and occasionally go apple picking but then end up with way too much fruit and not enough apple recipes.

Serves 4 to 6
Prep time: 5 minutes
Cook time: 25 minutes
Blade: A

2 or 3 apples, cored and spiralized

1 tablespoon grass-fed butter, melted

Ground cinnamon, for sprinkling

1. Preheat the oven to 325°F.

2. Trim the spiralized apples into 1- to 2-inch pieces, and spread them out on a large baking sheet in a single layer.

3. Drizzle the melted butter over the apples, and sprinkle them with cinnamon. Toss gently with your hands to combine, then spread them back out again.

4. Bake for 20 to 25 minutes, or until the apples have dried out slightly.

5. Remove from the oven, allow to cool, and serve.

TIP: Use coconut oil instead of butter to make this recipe vegan.

PER SERVING Calories: 112; Saturated Fat: 2g; Total Fat: 3g; Protein: 1g; Total Carbs: 23g; Fiber: 4g; Sodium: 22mg

Spiralized Fruit Salad

NO COOK • ONE POT • PALEO • VEGAN

I love this simple fruit salad because it incorporates some fruit noodles, which are so fun! It's a delicious combination of cantaloupe and apple noodles with fresh berries, lemon juice, and a little chopped mint for extra brightness. Bring this to your next summer potluck and impress everyone with a new take on a classic.

Serves 4 to 6
Prep time: 10 minutes
Blade: B, C, and/or D

1 spiralized cantaloupe (peel cantaloupe and spiralize whole until seeds show, then scoop them out and continue spiralizing)

2 or 3 apples, spiralized

1 cup raspberries

1 cup blackberries

2 tablespoons freshly squeezed lemon juice

¼ cup chopped fresh mint

In a large bowl, combine the cantaloupe, apples, raspberries, blackberries, lemon juice, and mint. Toss gently. Serve right away or refrigerate until ready to serve, up to 2 days.

TIP: Add some chopped nuts to this salad for an extra boost of fat and crunch factor.

PER SERVING Calories: 160; Saturated Fat: 0g; Total Fat: 1g; Protein: 3g; Total Carbs: 40g; Fiber: 9g; Sodium: 23mg

Spiralized Sweet Potato Chips

5-INGREDIENT • ONE POT • PALEO • VEGAN

This baked sweet potato chip recipe uses the ribbon noodle blade for spiralizing, so it kind of creates a mash-up of sliced chips and curly fries. It's the best of both worlds! I love spiralizing sweet potatoes because it goes so much faster than slicing them by hand, and I find that they cook a lot faster in the oven this way, too. Serve with a little ketchup or garlic aioli and you've got a delicious snack anytime.

Serves 2 to 4
Prep time: 5 minutes
Cook time: 25 minutes
Blade: A

2 large sweet potatoes, peeled and spiralized

2 tablespoons olive oil

Salt

Freshly ground black pepper

1. Preheat the oven to 400°F.

2. Trim the sweet potato noodles into 1- to 2-inch pieces, and spread them out on a large baking sheet.

3. Drizzle with the olive oil and season with salt and pepper. Use your hands to toss everything together until the sweet potato noodles are well-coated with oil and seasoned evenly, then spread the sweet potatoes back into an even layer.

4. Bake for 20 to 25 minutes, or until they've softened and the edges are beginning to brown.

5. Remove from the oven and serve immediately.

TIP: Sweet potatoes are never keto, but you can add fat and protein and turn this into more of a main dish by topping with your favorite chili, cheese, and some sour cream.

PER SERVING Calories: 232; Saturated Fat: 2g; Total Fat: 14g; Protein: 2g; Total Carbs: 26g; Fiber: 4g; Sodium: 149mg

Cucumber Noodle Salad with Watermelon and Feta

5-INGREDIENT • NO COOK • ONE POT • VEGETARIAN

This salad with cucumber and watermelon is perfect for summer—one of my friends brought something similar to a Fourth of July barbecue last year and it was so delicious. I can't get enough of the amazing combination of crunchy cucumber, sweet watermelon, and salty feta cheese, plus a generous sprinkle of fresh mint. Spiralizing the cucumber instead of dicing it adds some nice texture variation, as well.

Serves 4 to 6
Prep time: 10 minutes
Blade: C

2 large cucumbers, spiralized

½ large watermelon, diced

About 6 ounces crumbled feta cheese

Olive oil, for drizzling

Balsamic vinegar, for drizzling

Salt

Freshly ground black pepper

¼ cup fresh chopped mint, plus more for garnish

1. In a large bowl, combine the cucumber noodles, watermelon, and feta cheese. Toss to combine, and drizzle with a little olive oil and vinegar. Season with salt and pepper.

2. Add the mint and toss to combine. Serve topped with more fresh mint. Serve immediately or refrigerate for a few hours until ready to serve.

TIP: If you don't have or enjoy watermelon, you could use sliced strawberries instead. Make this salad vegan and Paleo by omitting the feta cheese.

PER SERVING Calories: 253; Saturated Fat: 7g; Total Fat: 13g; Protein: 9g; Total Carbs: 30g; Fiber: 3g; Sodium: 522mg

Caprese Veggie Noodle Pasta Salad

5-INGREDIENT · NO COOK · ONE POT · VEGETARIAN

One of my favorite salads is also one of the simplest—just sliced tomatoes, mozzarella, lots of fresh basil, and some olive oil drizzled on top. I used to have it as a sandwich all the time, but since going Paleo and then keto I've skipped the bread and just made little stacks that I enjoy on their own. This one is more of a salad, with spiralized summer squash or zucchini, so you can enjoy it as a snack, appetizer, or even a side dish with dinner.

Serves 4
Prep time: 10 minutes
Blade: A

2 large summer squash or zucchini, spiralized

1½ cups cherry tomatoes, halved

16 ounces mozzarella, cut into slices (you could get little balls if you prefer)

¼ cup olive oil

1 garlic clove, minced

Salt

Freshly ground black pepper

½ cup chopped fresh basil

1. In a large bowl, combine the summer squash noodles, cherry tomatoes, and mozzarella.

2. Add the olive oil and garlic. Season with salt and pepper and toss gently to combine. Add the basil and serve immediately.

TIP: If you want to add some meat to this dish, mix in 8 to 10 ounces of chopped prosciutto.

PER SERVING Calories: 425; Saturated Fat: 13g; Total Fat: 31g; Protein: 29g; Total Carbs: 9g; Fiber: 2g; Sodium: 753mg

Spiralized Potato Salad

5-INGREDIENT · DAIRY-FREE

This spiralized potato salad is a fun combination of traditional potato salad and pasta salad, since the potatoes are made into noodles. I like to throw some green beans into the mix to up the veggie content. Green beans and potatoes are kind of a classic combination, and they're especially delicious with a little bacon.

Serves 4
Prep time: 5 minutes
Cook time: 10 minutes
Blade: B or C

2 cups chopped green beans

2 large russet potatoes, spiralized

4 to 6 cooked bacon slices, diced

¼ cup mayonnaise

1 tablespoon mustard

Salt

Freshly ground black pepper

1. Bring a large stockpot of water to a boil. Cook the green beans until crisp-tender, about 5 minutes, then use a slotted spoon to transfer them to a large bowl of ice water. Drain and set aside.

2. Add the potato noodles to the same pot of boiling water and cook for 2 to 3 minutes until slightly softened. Remove from the heat and drain.

3. In a large bowl, combine the cooked potato noodles with the green beans and bacon. Add the mayonnaise and mustard and toss gently to combine. Season with salt and pepper and serve immediately, or refrigerate until ready to serve.

TIP: Skip the bacon to make this potato salad vegetarian.

PER SERVING Calories: 315; Saturated Fat: 5g; Total Fat: 18g; Protein: 14g; Total Carbs: 26g; Fiber: 5g; Sodium: 811mg

Spiralized Veggie Spring Rolls

NO COOK • VEGAN

Spring rolls are one of my all-time favorite light lunches, and I only recently started making them on my own. I was so pleasantly surprised to learn not only how easy they are to do at home, but how fun they can be. For at least a week I couldn't stop making them and kept inviting friends over to eat them. I don't think anyone minded. I love mine stuffed with shrimp, but here we leave it out to make these rolls vegan.

Serves 2 to 4
Prep time: 20 minutes
Blade: D

FOR THE SPRING ROLLS

4 to 6 rice paper/spring roll wrappers

¼ to ½ head iceberg lettuce, chopped

Handful fresh mint, chopped

4 to 6 fresh basil leaves

2 or 3 cilantro sprigs

1 small spiralized zucchini (to take the place of what is traditionally vermicelli)

1 spiralized carrot

½ spiralized cucumber

FOR THE DIPPING SAUCE

1 tablespoon garlic-chili sauce

3 to 4 tablespoons hoisin sauce

Juice of ½ lime

2 to 3 tablespoons crushed peanuts

TO MAKE THE SPRING ROLLS

1. Assemble all the spring roll ingredients in one place so they're easy to access. I like spreading everything out on a large cutting board.

2. Fill a shallow bowl with warm water and place one spring roll wrapper in it. Allow it to soak for a couple of seconds, then pull it out and lay it flat.

3. Layer the lettuce, mint, basil, cilantro, zucchini noodles, and carrot in the center of the wrapper. Carefully roll it up, folding the ends inward to contain all the fillings. (Be careful not to over-stuff or you won't be able to get the wrapper closed!)

4. Repeat with the remaining rice paper and fillings.

TO MAKE THE DIPPING SAUCE

In a small bowl, combine the garlic-chili and hoisin sauces with the lime juice. Stir well, top with the crushed peanuts, and serve with the spring rolls.

TIP: Make these rolls keto-friendly by using lettuce wraps or collard green leaves instead of rice paper. For extra protein, add 4 to 6 ounces of cooked, sliced shrimp.

PER SERVING Calories: 352; Saturated Fat: 1g; Total Fat: 9g; Protein: 9g; Total Carbs: 48g; Fiber: 5g; Sodium: 754mg

Spiralized Veggie Fritters

DAIRY-FREE · KETO · PALEO · VEGETARIAN

These spiralized veggie fritters are a great way to use up any veggies that need to be cooked or eaten before they get too wilty or start to go bad. I like to use zucchini noodles, but you could also throw other veggies in there, like chopped broccoli or spiralized or grated carrots. Feel free to customize it depending on your tastes and what's in your refrigerator.

Serves 2 to 4
Prep time: 10 minutes
Cook time: 15 minutes
Blade: D

12 ounces fresh spinach, cooked and drained

1 large zucchini, spiralized and roughly chopped

6 scallions, chopped

2 or 3 garlic cloves, minced

2 large eggs, lightly beaten

½ cup almond flour

1 teaspoon salt

2 tablespoons olive oil, divided

1. Squeeze as much liquid out of the spinach as possible with your hands.

2. In a large bowl, combine the spinach, zucchini, scallions, and garlic.

3. Add the eggs, almond flour, and salt. Mix well.

4. In a large nonstick skillet over medium-high heat, heat 1 tablespoon of olive oil. Drop heaping tablespoons of the mixture into the hot pan. Cook for 3 to 4 minutes per side, flattening a little with your spatula to make them into thin fritters.

5. Repeat with the remaining 1 tablespoon of oil and the batter and serve hot.

TIP: Top these fritters with a little sour cream if you tolerate dairy and want to make them even more keto-friendly.

PER SERVING Calories: 309; Saturated Fat: 23g; Total Fat: 4g; Protein: 15g; Total Carbs: 16g; Fiber: 7g; Sodium: 1387mg

Spiralized Latkes

5-INGREDIENT • VEGETARIAN

These spiralized "latkes" are made with a technique similar to the veggie noodle buns in the breakfast and sandwich chapters. Instead of using grated potatoes in my latkes, I spiralize them for a quicker prep time. If you want, you can chop up the noodles to make them smaller, but I like to just trim them a bit with scissors and fry them up in little piles. For a real treat, garnish them with chopped scallion and a little dollop of sour cream.

Serves 2 to 4
Prep time: 5 minutes
Cook time: 25 minutes
Blade: D

3 or 4 white potatoes, peeled and spiralized

½ white onion, finely chopped

1 large egg, beaten

Salt

Freshly ground black pepper

½ cup olive oil

Sliced scallions and/or sour cream, for topping (both optional but encouraged)

1. In a large bowl, combine the potato noodles, onion, and egg. Season with salt and pepper, and toss to combine well.

2. In a large skillet over medium heat, heat the olive oil. Take a heaping spoonful of potato noodle mixture from the bowl and form it into a little patty in your hand. Carefully transfer it to the hot oil and fry for 4 to 6 minutes per side, or until the noodles have softened and the surface of the latke is browned. Repeat with the remaining potato noodles. Serve hot with the scallions and sour cream (if using).

TIP: To make these latkes Paleo, use sweet potatoes instead of white potatoes and leave off the sour cream.

PER SERVING Calories: 557; Saturated Fat: 5g; Total Fat: 28g; Protein: 11g; Total Carbs: 70g; Fiber: 11g; Sodium: 139mg

Veggie Noodle Primavera, *page 70*

Vegan & Vegetarian Mains

I was almost a vegetarian for a few years before going Paleo, but my diet at that time wasn't nearly as healthy as I think the word "vegetarian" often brings to mind (think lots of muffins and sugary lattes). But once I started incorporating more meat into my diet and cutting out the grains, I found that veggies started making their way in more easily as well; and once I bought a spiralizer, I would find myself making meat-free dishes without even thinking about it. In this chapter you'll find lots of great vegetarian dishes, including some that are vegan and even a few raw ones that don't require any cooking at all.

Veggie Noodle Wraps

NO COOK • VEGETARIAN

These wraps are an easy lunch or appetizer (you can cut them into slices and serve on a platter like little pinwheels), and using collard greens instead of lettuce really allows you to fill it up and wrap it up almost like a burrito. I love using ranch dressing in these, but if you want to boost the protein or change up the flavor, try a couple dollops of hummus instead.

Serves 2 to 4
Prep time: 20 minutes
Blade: D

2 to 4 large collard green leaves, washed and dried

1 carrot, spiralized

1 cucumber, spiralized

1 zucchini, spiralized

1 green or red bell pepper, spiralized

½ spiralized red onion

1 avocado, sliced

½ cup sprouts (optional)

2 to 4 tablespoons ranch dressing (homemade if possible)

Salt

Freshly ground black pepper

1. Lay out the collard green leaves on a flat surface, and trim and discard the large, tough bottoms of the stems.

2. Layer an equal amount of carrot, cucumber, zucchini, bell pepper, onion, avocado, and sprouts (if using) onto each leaf. Add a drizzle of ranch dressing, and season with salt and pepper. Wrap each into a burrito shape, tucking the ends in as you go. Secure with toothpicks and slice in half if desired. Serve immediately.

TIP: If you aren't vegetarian, add some deli turkey or ham to up the protein in these wraps, and use a dairy-free dressing to make them Paleo and dairy-free.

PER SERVING Calories: 288; Saturated Fat: 4g; Total Fat: 20g; Protein: 6g; Total Carbs: 27g; Fiber: 11g; Sodium: 289mg

Cold Peanut Noodles

NO COOK • ONE POT • VEGAN

If you read my blog or have flipped through any of my other cookbooks, you know I'm a sucker for Asian food in general, but particularly Pad Thai. It's my go-to cheat meal, but these cold peanut veggie noodles do a really good job keeping me from getting Thai takeout every time a craving hits me. This is a salad that makes you feel like you're having noodles, so you can enjoy it any time you find yourself daydreaming about noodles and peanut sauce.

Serves 2 to 4
Prep time: 10 minutes
Blade: C

⅓ cup smooth peanut butter

¼ cup gluten-free soy sauce

2 tablespoons rice vinegar

Salt

Freshly ground black pepper

2 large zucchini, spiralized

2 or 3 carrots, spiralized

½ red bell pepper, spiralized

2 or 3 scallions, chopped

¼ cup chopped fresh cilantro

2 to 3 tablespoons chopped peanuts (optional)

1. In a large bowl, combine the peanut butter, soy sauce, and vinegar, and season with salt and pepper. Whisk thoroughly to combine until completely smooth. (If you don't care too much about keeping this a one-pot dish, you could even blend this in a blender and then pour over the veggies.)

2. Add the zucchini, carrots, and bell pepper noodles to the dressing. Toss well to combine. Add the scallions, and give it another stir.

3. Serve topped with the cilantro and chopped peanuts (if using).

TIP: Make this dish Paleo-friendly by substituting almond butter and chopped almonds for peanut butter and chopped peanuts.

PER SERVING Calories: 369; Saturated Fat: 5g; Total Fat: 22g; Protein: 17g; Total Carbs: 31g; Fiber: 8g; Sodium: 1970mg

Chilled Sesame Noodles

NO COOK · ONE POT · VEGAN

These chilled noodles are one of my favorite things to eat in the summer. They take no time at all and are done in 10 minutes or less. I absolutely love the crunch of cucumber noodles—I actually think cucumbers are my favorite vegetable to spiralize! I'm also partial to any recipe that can be thrown together in a bowl, tossed to combine, and eaten with chopsticks, so this one is at the top of my list.

Serves 2 to 4
Prep time: 10 minutes
Blade: B

2 spiralized cucumbers

8 ounces extra-firm tofu, cut into 1-inch cubes

¼ cup gluten-free soy sauce

2 to 3 tablespoons sesame oil

2 tablespoons rice vinegar

1 garlic clove, minced

Sliced scallions, for garnish

Sesame seeds, for garnish (optional)

1. In a large bowl, combine the cucumber noodles and tofu.

2. Add the soy sauce, sesame oil, rice vinegar, and garlic to the bowl and toss well to combine.

3. Transfer into serving bowls, top with scallions and sesame seeds (if using), and serve.

TIP: Add ½ pound of cooked and chilled shrimp to this recipe if you aren't vegetarian or vegan.

PER SERVING Calories: 358; Saturated Fat: 4g; Total Fat: 27g; Protein: 15g; Total Carbs: 16g; Fiber: 2g; Sodium: 1812mg

Zucchini Noodles with Vegan Avocado Cream Sauce

5-INGREDIENT · NO COOK · KETO · PALEO · VEGAN

This vegan avocado cream sauce is fantastic on almost anything, but I especially enjoy it tossed into raw zucchini noodles for a quick vegan lunch or side dish. You can make the sauce in the blender and refrigerate it for up to a day before using, or you can whip it up as needed.

Serves 2 to 4
Prep time: 15 minutes
Blade: C

1 large, ripe avocado, halved

¼ cup full-fat canned coconut milk

2 tablespoons olive oil

Juice of 1 lime

¼ teaspoon cayenne pepper (optional)

Salt

Freshly ground black pepper

2 or 3 large zucchini, spiralized

1. In a blender, combine the avocado, coconut milk, olive oil, lime juice, and cayenne pepper (if using). Blend until smooth, and season with salt and pepper.

2. Toss the zucchini noodles in a large bowl with as much of the avocado sauce as desired. Mix well to combine and serve immediately.

TIP: Make this dish extra special with a squeeze of fresh lime or some chopped fresh cilantro. If you aren't counting carbs, try this sauce over raw carrot noodles or sautéed sweet potato noodles for a non-keto but still Paleo variation.

PER SERVING Calories: 447; Saturated Fat: 13g; Total Fat: 41g; Protein: 6g; Total Carbs: 22g; Fiber: 11g; Sodium: 118mg

Greek Pasta Salad

NO COOK • ONE POT • KETO • VEGETARIAN

Pasta salad was one of those things I never really thought about. About a year after I decided to cut grains out of my diet, my friend made some at the beach and I couldn't believe how good it looked. This is a veggie-packed take on a Greek pasta salad, and it's a quick, easy, and super delicious way to incorporate veggie noodles. Since these noodles don't have to be cooked, you'll have it ready in minutes, too.

Serves 4
Prep time: 20 minutes
Blade: A

½ cup olive oil

¼ cup red wine vinegar

1 garlic clove, minced

1 tablespoon dried oregano

Salt

Freshly ground black pepper

2 large zucchini, spiralized

½ cup cherry tomatoes, halved

½ red onion, chopped (or spiralized on blade D, then roughly chopped)

½ red bell pepper, spiralized

½ green bell pepper, spiralized

½ cucumber, spiralized

½ cup crumbled feta cheese

¼ cup sliced black olives

1. In a large bowl, whisk the olive oil, vinegar, garlic, and oregano. Season with salt and pepper.

2. Add the zucchini, cherry tomatoes, onion, red and green bell peppers, and cucumber to the bowl and toss to combine with the dressing. Add the feta cheese and olives, then season again with salt and pepper.

3. Serve immediately or store (covered) in the refrigerator until ready to serve.

TIP: Make this recipe dairy-free and Paleo-friendly by skipping the feta. If you want to keep it keto and dairy-free, add some sliced avocado. Leftovers will keep in the refrigerator for up to three days.

PER SERVING Calories: 323; Saturated Fat: 7g; Total Fat: 31g; Protein: 5g; Total Carbs: 12g; Fiber: 3g; Sodium: 335mg

Veggie Noodle Pasta Salad with Goat Cheese, Almonds, and Cranberries

NO COOK · ONE POT · VEGETARIAN

This salad is lovely to serve in the fall—summer squash is so pretty when spiralized with the ribbon noodle blade, and it's even nicer when paired with tangy goat cheese, crunchy almonds, and dried cranberries. Bring this to your next holiday potluck, and I'll bet everyone will ask you for the recipe.

Serves 2 to 4
Prep time: 15 minutes
Blade: A and D

½ cup olive oil

¼ cup balsamic vinegar

1 tablespoon Dijon mustard

1 garlic clove, minced

Salt

Freshly ground black pepper

2 or 3 summer squash, spiralized

2 or 3 carrots, spiralized (use blade D)

6 ounces crumbled goat cheese

¼ cup dried, unsweetened cranberries

¼ cup slivered almonds, for serving

1. In a large bowl, combine the olive oil, balsamic vinegar, Dijon mustard, and garlic. Whisk well until smooth and combined. Season with salt and pepper.

2. Add the squash and carrot noodles, and toss to combine. Add the goat cheese and cranberries and stir gently. Top with the slivered almonds and serve right away.

TIP: Omit the goat cheese if you're dairy-free or Paleo.

PER SERVING Calories: 842; Saturated Fat: 18g; Total Fat: 72g; Protein: 16g; Total Carbs: 23g; Fiber: 7g; Sodium: 575mg

Potato Noodles with Mushrooms and Sage

ONE POT • VEGETARIAN

I made this recipe for the first time last fall and it quickly became a favorite. There's something so incredibly comforting about potato noodles—they have the starchy goodness of gnocchi but still maintain the consistency of traditional pasta, and all without any grains. White potatoes aren't included in a strict Paleo diet, but if you follow a Whole30-style diet you can have them, provided you prepare them yourself without a bunch of non-Paleo oils or additives. This recipe is perfect for those times when you want to indulge but would like to stick to your diet at the same time.

Serves 2
Prep time: 5 minutes
Cook time: 20 minutes
Blade: D

3 tablespoons grass-fed butter, divided

1 tablespoon olive oil

8 to 10 ounces button or cremini mushrooms, sliced

2 or 3 garlic cloves, minced

3 fresh sage leaves, chopped

Salt

Freshly ground black pepper

1 large russet potato, peeled and spiralized

1½ cups water or broth

Grated Parmesan cheese, for serving (optional)

1. In a large skillet over medium heat, heat 2 tablespoons of butter with the olive oil. Add the mushrooms and stir. Add the garlic. Spread out the mushrooms so they're all making even contact with the skillet surface. Allow to cook until browned, stirring occasionally, 6 to 8 minutes.

2. Add the sage leaves, and season with salt and pepper, stirring to combine everything well. Remove the mushroom mixture from the skillet and set aside.

3. Add the potato noodles to the skillet with the remaining 1 tablespoon of butter. Cook for 5 to 7 minutes, then add the water. Reduce the heat to medium-low and stir. Season with salt and pepper, and simmer for 2 to 3 minutes.

4. To serve, transfer the potato noodles into bowls and top with the mushrooms. Finish with a sprinkle of Parmesan (if using).

TIP: Make this recipe low-carb, strict Paleo, and keto-friendly by using spiralized summer squash instead of potato, and leave off the cheese. Follow the recipe as written but cook the noodles for only 3 to 4 minutes, or until fork-tender.

PER SERVING Calories: 323; Saturated Fat: 12g; Total Fat: 25g; Protein: 6g; Total Carbs: 22g; Fiber: 3g; Sodium: 215mg

Lemon-Garlic Zucchini Noodles

5-INGREDIENT · NO COOK · PALEO · VEGAN

Zucchini is a vegetable that I never thought to eat raw until I started spiralizing—there's something about putting it in noodle form that makes it appealing. It's quick and easy, and it keeps it nice and firm like regular pasta. It definitely needs vinaigrette or sauce, though, and that's where this lemon-garlic dressing comes in.

Serves 2 to 4
Prep time: 10 minutes
Blade: D

Juice of 1 large lemon

1 garlic clove, finely minced

¼ to ½ cup olive oil

Salt

Freshly ground black pepper

2 large zucchini, spiralized

1. In a large bowl, combine the lemon juice and garlic. Whisk as you pour in the olive oil, then season with salt and pepper.

2. Add the zucchini noodles to the bowl, and toss well to combine. Serve right away or refrigerate for a few hours until ready to serve.

TIP: Make this a keto-friendly main course by adding some cooked shrimp.

PER SERVING Calories: 466; Saturated Fat: 7g; Total Fat: 51g; Protein: 3g; Total Carbs: 7g; Fiber: 2g; Sodium: 97mg

Veggie Noodle Primavera

ONE POT · VEGETARIAN

This is my favorite kind of meal—tons of veggies, mostly spiralized, which makes me feel like I'm really eating a big bowl of noodles. Once you have your vegetables prepped and spiralized, this dish comes together in under 10 minutes. I like mine barely sautéed, so all the veggies still have a nice bite to them.

Serves 4 to 6
Prep time: 15 minutes
Cook time: 10 minutes
Blade: C or D

¼ cup olive oil

4 garlic cloves, thinly sliced

3 carrots, spiralized or thinly sliced

1 red bell pepper, spiralized or thinly sliced

½ cup broccoli florets

½ cup cherry tomatoes, halved

Salt

Freshly ground black pepper

1 large zucchini, spiralized

2 yellow squash, spiralized

¼ teaspoon red pepper flakes

½ cup chopped fresh basil

¼ cup grated Parmesan cheese (optional)

1. In a large skillet over medium-high heat, heat the olive oil. Sauté the garlic for 1 to 2 minutes until fragrant. Add the carrot and bell pepper noodles, broccoli, and cherry tomatoes and stir gently. Allow to cook for 3 to 4 minutes until the noodles begin to become tender. Season with salt and pepper.

2. Add the zucchini and yellow squash noodles. Toss everything together and cook for another 3 to 4 minutes. Add the red pepper flakes, and season again with salt and pepper.

3. Remove from the heat. Add the basil and Parmesan (if using), toss one last time, and serve.

TIP: Add some meat to this dish if you aren't a vegetarian—about 1 pound of diced chicken breast should do it (you can cook it in the pan before you start adding your veggies or just add some already cooked before serving).

PER SERVING Calories: 170; Saturated Fat: 2g; Total Fat: 13g; Protein: 3g; Total Carbs: 14g; Fiber: 4g; Sodium: 100mg

Zucchini Noodle Pomodoro

ONE POT • PALEO • VEGETARIAN

Maybe I'm just a kid at heart, but I don't think there's anything better than pasta with a simple and delicious red sauce. This recipe replaces traditional spaghetti with spiralized zucchini, but the red sauce is just as good as it always was.

Serves 2 to 4
Prep time: 5 minutes
Cook time: 20 minutes
Blade: D

2 tablespoons olive oil

1 onion, chopped

3 or 4 garlic cloves, minced

Salt

Freshly ground black pepper

¼ teaspoon red pepper flakes (more or less depending on heat preference)

1 (28-ounce) can crushed tomatoes (no sugar added)

2 tablespoons grass-fed butter

2 or 3 large zucchini, spiralized

¼ cup grated Parmesan cheese, for serving

Chopped fresh basil, for garnish

1. In a large saucepan over medium heat, heat the olive oil. Sauté the onion and garlic for 2 to 3 minutes, or until the garlic becomes fragrant and the onion begins to soften. Season with salt and pepper, and add the red pepper flakes.

2. Pour the tomatoes into the pot, and stir well to combine. (If desired, use an immersion blender or a regular blender to purée the sauce until smooth.) Season with salt and pepper. Reduce the heat to a simmer and allow to cook for at least 10 minutes.

3. About 5 minutes before you're ready to serve, add the butter to the sauce and stir until melted. Add the zucchini noodles and toss gently to combine. Cook for 2 to 3 minutes more, then serve immediately, topped with the Parmesan and basil.

TIP: If you aren't a vegetarian, add some meatballs to this dish to give it a bit more protein.

PER SERVING Calories: 387; Saturated Fat: 12g; Total Fat: 30g; Protein: 11g; Total Carbs: 27g; Fiber: 7g; Sodium: 667mg

Cacio e Pepe

5-INGREDIENT • ONE POT • KETO • VEGETARIAN

"Cacio e pepe" means "cheese and pepper" in Italian, and that's exactly what it is—pasta in a deliciously simple, peppery cheese sauce. With olive oil and butter and plenty of Pecorino Romano, this is an extremely luxurious dish that you can throw together in way less than 30 minutes, and with only a handful of ingredients. I like using summer squash noodles for this dish, but you could use zucchini or any other spiralizable veggie you might have in your refrigerator.

Serves 2 to 4
Prep time: 5 minutes
Cook time: 10 minutes
Blade: C

¼ cup olive oil

Plenty of freshly ground black pepper (to your liking but less than a tablespoon)

2 tablespoons grass-fed butter

1 cup very finely grated Pecorino Romano, plus more for serving

3 or 4 summer squash, spiralized

Salt

1. In a large skillet over medium-low heat, heat the olive oil and black pepper until the pepper is barely starting to sizzle, about 1 minute.

2. Add the butter, stirring continuously as it melts. Add the cheese, stirring until melted and well combined, about 5 minutes—you want the sauce smooth, not clumpy or oily in any way.

3. Add the squash noodles and cook for 2 to 3 minutes, or until fork-tender.

4. Season with salt and serve right away, topped with more cheese if desired.

TIP: For a non-vegetarian dish with a little extra flavor, add some chopped bacon as a topping.

PER SERVING Calories: 600; Saturated Fat: 21g; Total Fat: 53g; Protein: 23g; Total Carbs: 15g; Fiber: 4g; Sodium: 878mg

Veggie Pasta alla Norma

ONE POT • KETO • VEGETARIAN

Pasta alla Norma is a delicious Italian pasta dish loaded with eggplant, oregano, and lots of fresh basil and deliciously salty cheese. Zucchini and eggplant are a great combination, and I especially like the eggplant cubed and tossed into tender zucchini noodles—it's a lot more fun than chopping everything up and roasting it in the oven, which is how I used to cook most of my vegetables before I discovered spiralizing.

Serves 2 to 4
Prep time: 5 minutes
Cook time: 25 minutes
Blade: B

¼ cup olive oil

1 large eggplant, cut into 1-inch dice

Salt

Freshly ground black pepper

3 garlic cloves, minced

1 teaspoon dried oregano

1 (28-ounce) can crushed tomatoes

2 or 3 large zucchini, spiralized

1 large bunch fresh basil, chopped

6 ounces grated Parmesan cheese

1. In a large skillet over medium-high heat, heat the olive oil. Brown the eggplant (you might have to do this in two batches to avoid overcrowding), turning so all sides turn a rich brown, 5 to 7 minutes. Season liberally with salt and pepper, then add the garlic and oregano.

2. Add the tomatoes and bring to a simmer. Reduce the heat to medium-low and cook for 10 to 15 minutes.

3. Add the zucchini noodles to the skillet 3 to 4 minutes before you're ready to serve.

4. Season again with salt and pepper, then top with the basil and Parmesan to serve.

TIP: Add a pound of ground beef to this recipe (and omit the cheese) to make it Paleo. Cook the beef after the eggplant, with more garlic and olive oil, for 5 to 7 minutes or until browned.

PER SERVING Calories: 617; Saturated Fat: 16g; Total Fat: 45g; Protein: 34g; Total Carbs: 30g; Fiber: 12g; Sodium: 997mg

Fettuccini Alfredo

5-INGREDIENT · KETO · VEGETARIAN

There's something so incredibly comforting about fettuccini Alfredo—it reminds me of being a kid in the best way. It's also easy to make at home, and when you substitute veggie noodles for regular pasta you can indulge as much as you want without all the excess carbs. This is one recipe where you need to take the time to salt the zucchini noodles so they don't water down the wonderful cheesy sauce.

Serves 2 to 4
Prep time: 20 minutes
Cook time: 10 minutes
Blade: B

2 or 3 large zucchini, spiralized

2 to 3 tablespoons salt

4 tablespoons (½ stick) grass-fed butter

1 cup heavy (whipping) cream

1 garlic clove, minced

1½ cups grated Parmesan cheese, plus more for serving

Salt

Freshly ground black pepper

1. In a colander, toss the zucchini noodles with the salt. Let drain for 20 minutes.

2. In a large saucepan over medium-low heat, melt the butter. Add the cream and simmer for 3 to 5 minutes.

3. Add the garlic and Parmesan, whisking to combine. Season with salt and pepper.

4. Rinse the zucchini noodles, drain well, and blot them dry. Add the noodles to the sauce and cook for 2 to 3 minutes, just until fork-tender.

5. Serve hot with more Parmesan on top, if desired.

TIP: Add ½ pound of diced chicken breast to this recipe to make it more keto-friendly instead of vegetarian.

PER SERVING Calories: 937; Saturated Fat: 54g; Total Fat: 86g; Protein: 34g; Total Carbs: 17g; Fiber: 3g; Sodium: 2191mg

Lemony Broccoli Noodles with Roasted Red Peppers

5-INGREDIENT • ONE POT • PALEO • VEGAN

I love spiralizing broccoli noodles—you use the stem, so it always kind of feels like bonus vegetables because I almost always used to throw that part away. I like using the florets and the broccoli stem noodles together in this savory and scrumptious recipe with a lemony pan sauce and rich, roasted red peppers.

Serves 2 to 4
Prep time: 5 minutes
Cook time: 15 minutes
Blade: D

1 garlic clove, minced

¼ cup olive oil

2 heads broccoli, florets removed and stems spiralized

6 ounces oil-packed roasted red peppers, drained and chopped

Salt

Freshly ground black pepper

Juice of 1 large lemon

1. In a large skillet over medium heat, sauté the garlic in the olive oil for 2 minutes, or until fragrant. Turn the heat up to medium-high, add the broccoli florets, toss to combine, and cook for 5 minutes more.

2. Add the broccoli noodles and cook for an additional 6 to 7 minutes until fork-tender. Add the roasted red peppers, and toss gently to combine.

3. Season everything with salt and pepper, then remove from the heat and add the lemon juice. Serve immediately.

TIP: Make this recipe keto-friendly by adding ¼ cup of heavy (whipping) cream instead of lemon juice. Top with ½ cup of shredded white Cheddar or Monterey Jack cheese.

PER SERVING Calories: 364; Saturated Fat: 4g; Total Fat: 27g; Protein: 11g; Total Carbs: 29g; Fiber: 10g; Sodium: 288mg

Vegan Veggie Noodle Mac and Cheese

5-INGREDIENT · PALEO · VEGAN

When I was writing this book, I asked around Facebook to see what recipes people love but wish they could make healthier, and the number one answer was macaroni and cheese. I understand why—it's comforting and delicious and easy to throw together, and is there anyone out there who doesn't love it? This recipe uses veggie noodles instead of pasta and cashews instead of cheese, so hopefully you'll find something to love about it, whether you're low-carb, Paleo, vegan, or some combination of them all!

Serves 2 or 3
Prep time: 5 minutes
Cook time: 20 minutes
Blade: B

¾ cup raw cashews

2 cups almond milk

2 tablespoons olive oil

¼ cup nutritional yeast

2 teaspoons onion powder

2 teaspoons garlic powder

Salt

Freshly ground black pepper

2 large zucchini, spiralized

1. In a food processor or blender, pulse the cashews into a powder—stop before they become cashew butter. In a saucepan over medium-high heat, combine the cashew powder with the almond milk and olive oil, stirring for 8 to 10 minutes until well combined.

2. Stir in the nutritional yeast, onion powder, and garlic powder. Season with salt and pepper. Reduce the heat to low and simmer for 8 to 10 more minutes, or until thickened slightly.

3. A few minutes before serving, add the zucchini noodles. Stir to combine and serve immediately.

TIP: For even thicker vegan mac and cheese, use potato noodles instead of zucchini.

PER SERVING Calories: 655; Saturated Fat: 6g; Total Fat: 45g; Protein: 30g; Total Carbs: 42g; Fiber: 14g; Sodium: 295mg

Spiralized Potato Crust Pizza

VEGETARIAN

I enjoy pizza so much, but gluten really bothers me most of the time. I try to avoid spending extra money on gluten-free crusts, so I love making this spiralized potato crust pizza at home. Not only is it gluten-free, but it's grain-free as well, which makes it Paleo-friendly (except for the cheese, which you can easily omit if you're sensitive to it). You can customize the toppings on these pizzas however you like, but I prefer them with some pizza sauce, mozzarella, and mushrooms or pepperoni. So delicious!

Serves 4
Prep time: 5 minutes
Cook time: 25 minutes
Blade: D

2 tablespoons olive
oil, divided

2 potatoes, peeled and
spiralized

Salt

Freshly ground black pepper

2 large eggs, beaten

2 tablespoons garlic powder

1 tablespoon dried oregano

1 cup pizza sauce
(no sugar added)

1 cup shredded
mozzarella cheese

1. In an oven-safe skillet over medium-high heat, heat 1 tablespoon of olive oil. Sauté the potato noodles for 3 to 4 minutes until fork-tender. Season with salt and pepper and remove from the heat.

2. Transfer the noodles to a large bowl and allow to cool slightly. Add the eggs, garlic powder, and oregano. Toss to combine, and transfer to a large nonstick skillet. Press down firmly to create a "crust" with the noodles that's as thin as possible. (You might want to use a piece of parchment paper to do this.)

3. Preheat the oven to broil.

4. Place the skillet on the stove over medium-high heat. Cook the crust on one side for 5 to 7 minutes until lightly browned on the bottom. Slide the crust onto a large plate, pour the remaining 1 tablespoon of olive oil into the skillet, then flip the plate and slide the crust back into the skillet to cook on the other side for another 5 to 7 minutes until lightly browned.

5. Top the pizza crust with the sauce and mozzarella, then transfer to the broiler until the cheese has melted and the edges of the potatoes have browned slightly, 4 to 5 minutes.

6. Cut into four pieces and serve immediately.

TIP: Add pepperoni or sausage to add some meat to this dish, or you can make it Paleo-friendly, dairy-free, and vegan by skipping the mozzarella.

PER SERVING Calories: 242; Saturated Fat: 3g; Total Fat: 11g; Protein: 9g; Total Carbs: 28g; Fiber: 5g; Sodium: 356mg

Pan-Roasted Salmon with Lemon-Dill Squash Noodles, *page 84*

Fish & Seafood Mains

For a long time, I never made fish or any other seafood at home—it seemed a little intimidating, and I always worried that it would make my apartment smell like fish. Then I started experimenting with adding more seafood to our diets, and I realized my fears were unfounded. There are so many easy recipes out there, and it's really hard to mess up a piece of fish—most cook quickly and don't take much effort at all. Plus, if you're using high-quality, fresh seafood, you don't need to worry that it will smell bad. I hope these recipes encourage you to make more seafood at home for yourself and your family.

Ahi Tuna Steak over Chilled Cucumber Noodles

5-INGREDIENT · DAIRY-FREE · KETO · PALEO

I love making ahi tuna because it's an easy-to-cook protein that doesn't take a lot of time—in fact, it's best when served rare or medium-rare. Just make sure you're purchasing high-quality fish if you aren't planning to cook it all the way through. These seared ahi tuna steaks are great over lightly dressed cucumber noodles—the combination of sesame oil and rice vinegar is a bright and refreshing pairing.

Serves 2 to 4
Prep time: 10 minutes
Cook time: 5 minutes
Blade: C

2 (6-ounce) pieces ahi tuna
Salt
Freshly ground black pepper
2 tablespoons olive oil
2 large cucumbers, chilled and spiralized
3 tablespoons sesame oil
2 tablespoons rice vinegar
Sesame seeds, for garnish

1. Season the tuna steaks liberally with salt and pepper.

2. In a large skillet over medium heat, heat the olive oil. Sear the fish for 2 to 3 minutes per side until brown and crispy.

3. In a large bowl, combine the cucumber noodles with the sesame oil and rice vinegar. Toss to combine, and season with salt and pepper.

4. To serve, transfer the cucumber noodles to bowls. Slice the tuna and serve it immediately over the noodles, garnished with sesame seeds.

TIP: Make this recipe even more keto-friendly with some diced avocado.

PER SERVING Calories: 512; Saturated Fat: 5g; Total Fat: 36g; Protein: 36g; Total Carbs: 11g; Fiber: 2g; Sodium: 136mg

Avocado and Crab Salad with Cucumber Noodles

NO COOK • DAIRY-FREE • KETO • PALEO

Avocado and crab are so very good together, and if you're in a hurry you can use canned crab meat—it's incredibly easy (and a little cheaper). You can also buy fresh crab meat from the seafood counter of your local grocery store if you want, though—it's totally up to you! This salad is light and fresh and really fun served over crisp cucumber noodles, making it a perfect choice for a quick, healthy lunch.

Serves 2 to 4
Prep time: 15 minutes
Blade: C

8 to 10 ounces cooked crab meat

2 large avocados, diced

Salt

Freshly ground black pepper

2 or 3 large cucumbers, spiralized

¼ cup olive oil

Juice of 1 large lemon

1 garlic clove, minced

2 or 3 scallions, chopped

1. In a medium bowl, combine the crab meat and avocado. Toss gently to combine (try not to squish the avocado), and season with salt and pepper.

2. In a large bowl, toss the cucumber noodles together with the olive oil, lemon juice, and garlic. Season with salt and pepper, and add the scallions.

3. Give it another toss and transfer to bowls for serving. Top with the crab and avocado and enjoy immediately.

TIP: If you don't want to use crab, try cooked, chopped shrimp instead.

PER SERVING Calories: 835; Saturated Fat: 12g; Total Fat: 68g; Protein: 25g; Total Carbs: 39g; Fiber: 16g; Sodium: 998mg

Thai Seafood Noodle Salad

NO COOK • ONE POT • DAIRY-FREE • PALEO

This speedy salad incorporates precooked shrimp and lots of spiralized veggies with a tangy, spicy Thai vinaigrette. It's great on its own as a light lunch or as a side dish with a larger meal. The substitution of spiralized veggies instead of the traditional rice noodles keeps this recipe nutrient-packed and much lower in carbs.

Serves 2 to 4
Prep time: 15 minutes
Blade: B

Juice of 2 to 3 limes

3 tablespoons coconut aminos (or gluten-free soy sauce)

1 to 2 tablespoons chili-garlic sauce (more as needed)

1 tablespoon fish sauce

1 teaspoon sesame oil

2 garlic cloves, minced

1 large zucchini, spiralized

2 carrots, spiralized

1 green bell pepper, spiralized

1 red bell pepper, spiralized

½ pound cooked shrimp, peeled and deveined

½ cup fresh basil, chopped

½ cup fresh cilantro, chopped

¼ cup crushed almonds

1. In a large bowl, combine the lime juice, coconut aminos, chili-garlic sauce, fish sauce, sesame oil, and garlic. Whisk to combine.

2. Add the zucchini, carrot, and bell pepper noodles, and the shrimp to the dressing in the bowl. Toss together to ensure that everything is well combined.

3. Add the basil, cilantro, and crushed almonds, then transfer to serving plates or bowls and enjoy right away.

TIP: If you aren't concerned with keeping this recipe Paleo, substitute crushed peanuts for the almonds.

PER SERVING Calories: 323; Saturated Fat: 1g; Total Fat: 11g; Protein: 32g; Total Carbs: 26g; Fiber: 6g; Sodium: 1454mg

Chilled Veggie Noodle Salad with Asparagus and Shrimp

NO COOK • ONE POT • DAIRY-FREE • KETO • PALEO

Shrimp, asparagus, and fresh lemon combine to make a perfect meal for spring. Using precooked shrimp makes this recipe an easy one to just throw together and serve. I like to add some spiralized veggies like raw zucchini to add even more texture, flavor, and nutrition to this dish.

Serves 4
Prep time: 15 minutes
Blade: A

¼ cup olive oil

1 garlic clove, minced

Juice of 1 lemon

Salt

Freshly ground black pepper

1 pound chilled asparagus, trimmed and cut on the diagonal into ½-inch pieces

½ pound cooked shrimp, peeled and deveined

2 large zucchini, chilled and spiralized

¼ teaspoon red pepper flakes

Chopped fresh parsley, for garnish

1. In a large bowl, combine the olive oil, garlic, and lemon juice. Season with salt and pepper.

2. Add the asparagus, shrimp, and zucchini noodles. Toss well to combine. Season again with salt and pepper as needed, adding the red pepper flakes.

3. Serve immediately, garnished with parsley.

TIP: If you aren't counting carbs, add some additional crunch to this salad with 2 or 3 spiralized carrots.

PER SERVING Calories: 215; Saturated Fat: 2g; Total Fat: 14g; Protein: 17g; Total Carbs: 9g; Fiber: 4g; Sodium: 189mg

Pan-Roasted Salmon with Lemon-Dill Squash Noodles

ONE POT · DAIRY-FREE · KETO · PALEO

Salmon and dill are such a classic combination, made even better with fresh lemon. Add some sautéed summer squash noodles and you have a fresh, flavorful, healthy meal that comes together super fast.

Serves 2
Prep time: 10 minutes
Cook time: 15 minutes
Blade: B

2 tablespoons olive oil

1 garlic clove, minced

2 (6- to 8-ounce) pieces salmon

Salt

Freshly ground black pepper

2 or 3 large summer squash, spiralized

Juice of 1 large lemon

2 to 3 tablespoons chopped fresh dill

1. In a large skillet over medium heat, heat the olive oil. Sauté the garlic for 2 minutes, or until fragrant. Add the salmon and cook for 4 to 5 minutes per side until golden brown. The fish should flake easily with a fork when cooked through. Season with salt and pepper, then remove the fish from the skillet and set aside.

2. Add the squash noodles to the skillet, then add the lemon juice. Season with salt and pepper, then top with the dill.

3. Toss gently to combine and divide among serving plates. Top with the salmon and serve immediately.

TIP: This recipe would be great with chicken as well, or with a white fish like tilapia or cod.

PER SERVING Calories: 461; Saturated Fat: 4g; Total Fat: 27g; Protein: 44g; Total Carbs: 13g; Fiber: 4g; Sodium: 203mg

Black Pepper Daikon Noodles with Shrimp and Snow Peas

ONE POT • DAIRY-FREE • PALEO

These black pepper daikon noodles are a nice change from the sesame and peanut noodles that I make so often—sometimes I want more of a full meal than those snack/salad dishes, and this one is loaded with shrimp and snow peas, so you get plenty of protein and some green veggies as well. If you've never used daikon noodles, you're in for a treat. The radish-y bite they offer adds something special to Asian-inspired dishes like this one.

Serves 2 to 4
Prep time: 10 minutes
Cook time: 15 minutes
Blade: C

2 tablespoons sesame oil

2 garlic cloves, minced

¼ cup coconut aminos
(or gluten-free soy sauce)

3 tablespoons rice vinegar

2 tablespoons honey

¼ teaspoon red pepper flakes

2 or 3 large daikon radishes, peeled and spiralized

1 pound shrimp, peeled and deveined

6 ounces snow peas

Freshly ground black pepper

1. In a large skillet over medium-high heat, heat the sesame oil. Sauté the garlic for 1 to 2 minutes, or until fragrant. Add the coconut aminos, rice vinegar, honey, and red pepper flakes and stir well to combine.

2. Add the daikon noodles and sauté for 5 to 7 minutes until fork-tender, then add the shrimp to the skillet and cook until pink, about 3 minutes more. Finally add the snow peas and cook for 2 to 3 minutes.

3. Season with plenty of black pepper and serve hot.

TIP: If you can't find daikon or don't like it, use zucchini, carrot, or potato noodles, or skip the spiralizing and use cauliflower rice instead.

PER SERVING Calories: 472; Saturated Fat: 2g; Total Fat: 16g; Protein: 49g; Total Carbs: 31g; Fiber: 3g; Sodium: 304mg

Zucchini Noodle Puttanesca

ONE POT • KETO

Spaghetti puttanesca is full of flavor, packed with capers, olives, and anchovies. Even if you aren't a huge fan of anchovies, I encourage you to try this. They add a briny, pleasant depth of flavor to dishes like this one.

Serves 2 to 4
Prep time: 10 minutes
Cook time: 10 minutes
Blade: D

¼ cup olive oil

3 or 4 garlic cloves,
thinly sliced

4 to 6 anchovy fillets, finely
chopped

¼ cup sliced black olives

¼ cup capers, drained
and chopped

¼ teaspoon red pepper flakes

Salt

Freshly ground black pepper

1 (16- or 18-ounce) can or jar
crushed tomatoes
(no sugar added)

2 or 3 large zucchini,
spiralized

¼ cup grated Parmesan
cheese, for serving

1. In a large skillet over medium heat, heat the olive oil . Sauté the garlic for 2 minutes, or until fragrant. Add the anchovies, olives, capers, and red pepper flakes. Season with salt and pepper, and cook for another minute or two until fragrant.

2. Add the tomatoes and stir well to combine. Bring to a low simmer and cook for another 4 to 5 minutes. Add the zucchini noodles and cook for an additional 2 to 3 minutes until fork-tender.

3. Season with salt and pepper and serve hot, topped with the Parmesan.

TIP: Bump up the protein in this dish by adding one can of olive oil–packed tuna to the sauce. To make it Paleo, just omit the cheese.

PER SERVING Calories: 445; Saturated Fat: 6g; Total Fat: 32g; Protein: 16g; Total Carbs: 33g; Fiber: 8g; Sodium: 1394mg

Poached Tilapia over Veggie Noodles

ONE POT · DAIRY-FREE · PALEO

I love tilapia because it is mild in flavor and cooks quickly. It's an easy fish to buy frozen, too, so I always have some in the freezer. This recipe is one of my favorites, with lots of veggie noodles and quick-poached fish in a fragrant broth. If you are new to eating fish, this recipe is a great way to start.

Serves 2
Prep time: 10 minutes
Cook time: 15 minutes
Blade: D

2 tablespoons olive oil

2 garlic cloves, minced

½ white onion, spiralized

2 carrots, spiralized

1 red bell pepper, spiralized

Salt

Freshly ground black pepper

1 cup vegetable or chicken broth

2 (6-ounce) pieces tilapia

1 large zucchini, spiralized

1. In a large saucepan over medium heat, heat the olive oil. Sauté the garlic for 1 to 2 minutes, or until fragrant.

2. Add the onion and cook for 2 to 3 minutes before adding the carrot and bell pepper noodles. Sauté for another 3 to 4 minutes, or until the vegetables have softened slightly. Season with salt and pepper.

3. Pour the broth into the pan and bring to a low simmer. Add the tilapia and cook in the broth for 3 to 4 minutes, or until the fish has become completely opaque. Season again with salt and pepper.

4. Add the zucchini noodles and cook for another 2 to 3 minutes, then serve right away.

TIP: You can make this recipe in the oven instead of on the stove. Put all the ingredients in a 9-by-13-inch baking dish and cover with aluminum foil. Bake at 350°F for 10 to 15 minutes, or until the fish is cooked through and the veggies are tender.

PER SERVING Calories: 376; Saturated Fat: 3g; Total Fat: 18g; Protein: 39g; Total Carbs: 18g; Fiber: 4g; Sodium: 601mg

Veggie Linguine with Clams

ONE POT · DAIRY-FREE · PALEO

This recipe is a great go-to if you're short on time but want to impress your family or some unexpected dinner guests—it's basically just veggie noodles in garlic and olive oil with canned clams and lots of fresh parsley on top. I really love the flavor (and juice!) from canned clams, but if you wanted to make this an even fancier dish you could always use fresh ones in the shell.

Serves 2 or 3
Prep time: 10 minutes
Cook time: 10 minutes
Blade: C

2 tablespoons olive oil

2 garlic cloves, minced

1 to 2 (6.5-ounce) cans clams with juice (or about 2 dozen small, fresh clams)

¼ to ½ cup white wine or broth (only if using fresh clams)

2 large zucchini, spiralized

2 summer squash, spiralized

Salt

Freshly ground black pepper

¼ to ½ teaspoon red pepper flakes

3 or 4 scallions, sliced

Chopped fresh parsley, for garnish

1. In a large skillet over medium heat, heat the olive oil. Sauté the garlic for about 1 minute. Add the clams with their juices, and give it a stir. (If using fresh clams, add the wine along with the clams, then cover the pan and simmer for a few minutes. Discard any clams that don't open.)

2. Add the zucchini and squash noodles and sauté until tender, about 5 minutes. Gently stir to combine all the ingredients. Season with salt and pepper, and add the red pepper flakes. Remove from the heat and add the scallions.

3. Serve hot with a sprinkle of parsley.

TIP: Add some Parmesan for extra flavor if you aren't dairy-free. When buying canned clams, look for brands packed without preservatives or other additives for the healthiest choice. If you decide on fresh clams, soak them for 20 minutes and then scrub clean before using.

PER SERVING Calories: 484; Saturated Fat: 3g; Total Fat: 18g; Protein: 46g; Total Carbs: 26g; Fiber: 5g; Sodium: 304mg

Spicy Shrimp Marinara

ONE POT • DAIRY-FREE • PALEO

This spicy shrimp marinara is zesty and full of flavor. Shrimp and tomato sauce combine so well and make a nice lunch or dinner when served over veggie noodles. This sauce is great on its own, too, and it keeps well in the freezer, but I love it best with fresh shrimp and lots of spiralized veggies.

Serves 2 to 4
Prep time: 10 minutes
Cook time: 20 minutes
Blade: D

2 tablespoons olive oil

½ onion, diced

2 garlic cloves, minced

1 (28-ounce) can crushed tomatoes (no sugar added)

1 teaspoon dried oregano

¼ teaspoon red pepper flakes (more as needed)

¼ cup white wine (optional)

Salt

Freshly ground black pepper

1 pound shrimp, peeled and deveined

2 or 3 large zucchini, spiralized

Chopped fresh parsley, for garnish

1. In a large stockpot over medium heat, heat the olive oil. Sauté the onion for 2 to 3 minutes until fragrant. Add the garlic and stir for another minute, then add the tomatoes and bring to a low simmer. Add the oregano, red pepper flakes, and white wine (if using), and season with salt and pepper. Cook on low for about 10 minutes.

2. Add the shrimp and cook for 4 to 5 minutes, or until pink and opaque throughout.

3. About 2 to 3 minutes before serving, add the zucchini noodles. Garnish with parsley and serve hot.

TIP: Make this a meat sauce by using 1 pound of ground beef instead of shrimp. Add it to the pot after the garlic and olive oil and cook for 5 to 7 minutes, or until browned.

PER SERVING Calories: 537; Saturated Fat: 2g; Total Fat: 18g; Protein: 57g; Total Carbs: 44g; Fiber: 12g; Sodium: 894mg

Lobster Mac and Cheese with Butternut Squash Noodles

ONE POT

Is there anything better than lobster mac and cheese? If you've had it, you know that the answer to that question is "no." My husband and I went out for a nice dinner in San Francisco over the summer and decided to order a huge side of lobster mac and cheese. It was so good, but we felt so full afterward, I knew I had to find a way to lighten it up. This recipe is still loaded with cheese and lobster, but instead of macaroni we use butternut squash noodles, which makes it a gluten- and grain-free recipe.

Serves 2
Prep time: 10 minutes
Cook time: 20 minutes
Blade: B

2 tablespoons olive oil

1 butternut squash, spiralized

4 tablespoons (½ stick) grass-fed butter

¼ cup gluten-free flour

2 cups milk

2 cups shredded Cheddar cheese, plus ½ cup for topping

Meat from 2 cooked lobster tails, chopped

Salt

Freshly ground black pepper

Sliced scallions, for garnish

1. In a large oven-safe skillet over medium-high heat, heat the olive oil. Sauté the butternut squash noodles for 5 to 7 minutes, or until slightly softened. Remove from the skillet and set aside.

2. In the same skillet, melt the butter. Add the flour and stir until smooth, then add the milk, stirring to combine. Reduce the heat to medium-low and cook, stirring occasionally, for about 5 minutes.

3. Slowly add 2 cups of Cheddar to the simmering sauce, stirring continuously as it melts.

4. Preheat the oven to broil. Add the squash noodles and the lobster meat, and toss gently to combine. Season with salt and pepper, then top with the remaining ½ cup of cheese and pop it under the broiler for 2 to 3 minutes, or until the cheese has melted.

5. Garnish with scallions and serve hot.

TIP: Make this recipe lower carb by using summer squash or zucchini noodles instead of butternut squash noodles.

PER SERVING Calories: 1346; Saturated Fat: 50g; Total Fat: 91g; Protein: 49g; Total Carbs: 74g; Fiber: 10g; Sodium: 1740mg

Summary Squash Pasta with Lobster and Tomato

This dish just screams summer to me—summer squash noodles tossed together with luscious lobster meat, fresh tomatoes, and a good amount of butter. In 30 minutes, you'll be ready to grab a chilled glass of white wine, sit on your deck or patio, and enjoy an elegant, luxurious warm-weather dinner.

Serves 2 to 4
Prep time: 10 minutes
Cook time: 20 minutes
Blade: D

1 tablespoon olive oil

½ white onion, diced

2 garlic cloves, minced

1 cup cherry tomatoes

Salt

Freshly ground black pepper

3 tablespoons
grass-fed butter

3 or 4 large summer squash,
spiralized

Meat from 3 or 4 cooked
lobster tails, chopped

¼ teaspoon red pepper flakes

¼ cup grated Parmesan
cheese, for serving

1. In a large skillet over medium heat, heat the olive oil. Sauté the onion and garlic together for 4 to 5 minutes, or until the garlic is fragrant and the onion becomes translucent and begins to soften.

2. Add the tomatoes and cook for 3 to 4 minutes, allowing them to burst and crushing any that don't with the back of a wooden spoon. Season with salt and pepper.

3. Add the butter to the skillet and stir as it melts. Add the summer squash noodles and cook for 2 to 3 minutes, then add the lobster meat, sprinkle with the red pepper flakes, and continue to cook until everything is warmed through, 5 to 7 minutes. Season with salt and pepper.

4. Serve immediately with Parmesan sprinkled generously over each serving.

TIP: Use cooked crab meat, clams, or even shrimp if you don't feel like buying lobster, and just leave off the Parmesan cheese to make it Paleo.

PER SERVING Calories: 613; Saturated Fat: 15g; Total Fat: 31g; Protein: 66g;
Total Carbs: 21g; Fiber: 6g; Sodium: 1786mg

Seafood Veggie Pasta

ONE POT

This is almost like a cioppino recipe, although it's a bit simplified. Here we use zucchini, carrot, and summer squash noodles instead of pasta, and the classic flavors of a seafood stew make this hybrid dish a perennial favorite. I love the combination of firm white fish with shrimp, but you can also try adding fresh clams or mussels, or just choose one type of seafood. You can even make this dish Paleo and dairy-free by simply leaving out the Parmesan cheese.

Serves 2 to 4
Prep time: 10 minutes
Cook time: 15 minutes
Blade: C

2 tablespoons olive oil

½ onion, diced

2 or 3 carrots, spiralized

2 garlic cloves, minced

1 (16- or 18-ounce) can or jar diced tomatoes, with juice (no sugar added)

1 cup seafood stock

6 ounces diced white fish, like cod or tilapia

½ pound shrimp, deveined (shells on or off, depending on your preference)

Salt

Freshly ground black pepper

¼ teaspoon red pepper flakes

1 large zucchini, spiralized

1 or 2 summer squash, spiralized

Grated Parmesan cheese, for serving

Chopped fresh parsley, for garnish

1. In a large stockpot over medium heat, heat the olive oil. Sauté the onion, carrot noodles, and garlic for 2 to 3 minutes, or until the garlic is fragrant and the onion is softened slightly. Add the tomatoes and seafood stock, and bring to a low simmer.

2. Add the fish and shrimp, and cook until opaque, 5 to 7 minutes. Season with salt and pepper, and add the red pepper flakes. About 2 to 3 minutes before serving, add the zucchini and summer squash noodles.

3. Transfer to serving bowls or plates and top with plenty of Parmesan. Serve immediately, garnished with parsley.

TIP: If you decide to add clams or mussels to this recipe, add them to the pot with the onion, garlic, and carrot noodles. Cover the pot after you add the tomatoes and seafood stock, and simmer until they open. Be sure to discard any that don't open after cooking.

PER SERVING Calories: 486; Saturated Fat: 3g; Total Fat: 18g; Protein: 55g; Total Carbs: 31g; Fiber: 10g; Sodium: 552mg

Clam Chowder with Spiralized Potatoes and Carrots

ONE POT

Clam chowder is one of those dishes that I love to order when I'm out but never really made for myself at home because I thought it would be too much work. Spiralizing the ingredients makes all the prep and chopping so much faster! I love using potato noodles instead of diced potatoes in pretty much any situation, but especially in a soup like this one.

Serves 4
Prep time: 10 minutes
Cook time: 20 minutes
Blade: D

2 tablespoons
grass-fed butter

1 onion, spiralized

2 garlic cloves, minced

2 or 3 celery stalks,
thinly sliced

3 or 4 carrots, spiralized

2 cups seafood stock

1 bay leaf

Salt

Freshly ground black pepper

2 russet potatoes, peeled and
spiralized

2 cups half-and-half

3 or 4 (6-ounce) cans clams

Hot sauce, for serving

Chopped fresh parsley,
for garnish

1. In a large stockpot over medium heat, melt the butter. Sauté the onion and garlic for 2 to 3 minutes, or until the garlic is fragrant and the onion is softened slightly. Add the celery and carrot noodles, and cook for 2 minutes more. Pour the seafood stock in and bring to a simmer. Add the bay leaf, and season with salt and pepper.

2. Add the potato noodles, and cook for about 5 minutes. Add the half-and-half and the clams with their juices, and stir well to combine. Season again with salt and pepper. Cook for about 10 minutes over low heat.

3. Remove the bay leaf before serving. Ladle into bowls, top with a few dashes of hot sauce, and garnish with parsley. Serve immediately.

TIP: Make this a keto-friendly recipe by skipping the potatoes altogether.

PER SERVING Calories: 345; Saturated Fat: 13g; Total Fat: 21g; Protein: 10g; Total Carbs: 32g; Fiber: 5g; Sodium: 758mg

Chicken Pad Thai, *page 96*

7

Chicken & Turkey Mains

Chicken is the protein I use the most at home, and while I don't cook with turkey very often, the two meats are easy to swap in most recipes. If you like one more than the other, go ahead and substitute it! In this chapter you'll find lots of Asian-inspired recipes; a few healthier takes on classic dishes like chicken pot pie, chicken Parmesan, and chicken and rice casserole; and a few of my own creations, like a sweet potato noodle taco skillet. I hope it gives you a lot of ideas to switch up what can sometimes become mundane poultry and veggie combos.

Chicken Pad Thai

ONE POT • DAIRY-FREE • KETO

Pad Thai is one of my all-time favorite dishes, and it's super easy to make at home with veggies instead of traditional rice noodles. I've found through experimenting with veggies and limiting grains that as long as the flavor of something is good, you really won't miss the carbs, and this recipe is definitely a perfect example of that!

Serves 2 to 4
Prep time: 10 minutes
Cook time: 20 minutes
Blade: B

1 tablespoon sesame oil

¼ red onion, thinly sliced

1 teaspoon peeled minced fresh ginger

1 garlic clove, minced

1 pound boneless chicken breast or thigh, thinly sliced

Juice of 2 limes, plus 1 lime cut into wedges for garnish

1 to 2 tablespoons peanut butter

2 tablespoons gluten-free soy sauce

½ tablespoon fish sauce

2 large zucchini, spiralized

2 or 3 carrots, spiralized

1 cup bean sprouts

3 or 4 scallions, sliced

¾ cup crushed peanuts

Salt

Freshly ground black pepper

Chopped fresh cilantro, for garnish

1. In a large skillet over medium heat, heat the oil. Add the onion, ginger, and garlic, and stir. Cook for about 5 minutes until the onion is tender, stirring frequently. Add the chicken and cook for an additional 5 minutes.

2. Add the lime juice, peanut butter, soy sauce, and fish sauce.

3. Add the zucchini and carrot noodles to the sauce, and cook for 4 to 5 minutes until fork-tender. Add the bean sprouts and scallions, and cook for an additional 2 to 3 minutes.

4. Remove from the heat, top with the crushed peanuts, season with salt and pepper, and serve with a wedge of lime and cilantro.

TIP: Use almond butter and sliced almonds instead of peanut butter and peanuts to make this recipe Paleo; if you follow a strict Paleo plan, use coconut aminos instead of the gluten-free soy sauce.

PER SERVING Calories: 1054; Saturated Fat: 9g; Total Fat: 65g; Protein: 91g; Total Carbs: 42g; Fiber: 15g; Sodium: 2587mg

Broccoli Noodle Pad See Ew

ONE POT • DAIRY-FREE

Pad See Ew is another one of my favorite dishes—it's my go-to when I'm in the mood for Pad Thai but want something a little more savory and less sweet. It's great with chicken, and I love substituting broccoli noodles for the traditional flat, wide rice noodles. I use blade B, or the fettuccini one, which I think mimics the shape and texture of the noodles the best.

Serves 4
Prep time: 5 minutes
Cook time: 20 minutes
Blade: B

2 tablespoons vegetable oil

2 garlic cloves, minced

1 pound boneless chicken breast or thigh, thinly sliced

2 heads broccoli, florets removed and stems spiralized

2 tablespoons gluten-free soy sauce

2 tablespoons oyster sauce

2 tablespoons rice vinegar

Small splash water (2 tablespoons or less, if needed)

1 or 2 large eggs, lightly beaten

Salt

Freshly ground black pepper

1. In a large nonstick skillet over medium heat, heat the oil. Sauté the garlic for 1 to 2 minutes, or until fragrant. Add the chicken to the pan and cook until browned, 5 to 6 minutes.

2. Add the broccoli florets and cook for 3 to 4 minutes until crisp-tender, then add the broccoli noodles.

3. Pour in the soy sauce, oyster sauce, and rice vinegar. Stir well to combine, ensuring that all the ingredients are evenly coated in sauce. If necessary, thin the sauce with a little bit of water.

4. Move some of the contents of the skillet to the side and crack the eggs in, scrambling them right there in the skillet. Incorporate the scrambled eggs into the rest of the ingredients and continue to stir until all is combined and the eggs are done, about 5 minutes.

5. Taste and season with salt and pepper, if necessary. Serve right away.

TIP: Use sliced steak instead of chicken for a change of pace.

PER SERVING Calories: 275; Saturated Fat: 2g; Total Fat: 11g; Protein: 34g; Total Carbs: 11g; Fiber: 4g; Sodium: 700mg

Carrot Noodle Stir-Fry with Chicken

ONE POT · DAIRY-FREE · PALEO

I love making quick and easy stir-fries like this one—you cook your meat quickly and add veggies, and all the flavors blend together in a way that's so satisfying and delicious. You can switch up the flavors and herbs however you like, but my favorite stir-fries are made with lots of garlic, fresh ginger, onion, and a little sesame oil.

Serves 2 to 4
Prep time: 10 minutes
Cook time: 15 minutes
Blade: D

2 tablespoons sesame oil

1 onion, spiralized

1 garlic clove, minced

1 pound boneless chicken breast, diced

2 or 3 carrots, spiralized

1 head broccoli, florets removed and chopped, stem spiralized

1 green bell pepper, spiralized

1 (8-ounce) can water chestnuts, drained

1 teaspoon peeled minced fresh ginger

1 large zucchini, spiralized

2 or 3 tablespoons coconut aminos (or gluten-free soy sauce)

Sesame seeds, for garnish

1. In a large skillet over medium-high heat, heat the sesame oil. Sauté the onion and garlic for 2 to 3 minutes, or until the garlic is fragrant and the onion is softened slightly. Add the chicken and cook for 5 to 7 minutes, or until browned, stirring frequently.

2. Add the carrots, broccoli florets and noodles, bell pepper noodles, water chestnuts, and ginger. Stir well to combine. After 3 to 4 minutes, add the zucchini noodles and coconut aminos. Stir again, sautéing for an additional 2 to 3 minutes, until the zucchini noodles are fork-tender.

3. Transfer to serving bowls or plates, sprinkle with sesame seeds, and serve.

TIP: Make this recipe vegetarian by subbing tofu or a few scrambled eggs for the chicken.

PER SERVING Calories: 615; Saturated Fat: 2g; Total Fat: 20g; Protein: 54g; Total Carbs: 49g; Fiber: 12g; Sodium: 256mg

Teriyaki Chicken with Daikon Noodles

DAIRY-FREE • PALEO

Teriyaki sauce is kind of hard to find in a Paleo-friendly version because it's high in sugar. Fortunately, this coconut aminos–honey mixture does a really good job of capturing those flavors without too many additives.

Serves 2 to 4
Prep time: 10 minutes
Cook time: 15 minutes
Blade: C

¼ cup coconut aminos
(or gluten-free soy sauce)

¼ cup honey

2 tablespoons orange juice

1 tablespoon rice vinegar

1 teaspoon peeled minced
fresh ginger

1 teaspoon sesame oil

1 garlic clove, minced

¼ teaspoon red pepper flakes

1 pound boneless chicken
breast or thigh, diced

3 or 4 daikon radishes,
spiralized

Salt

Freshly ground black pepper

1. In a medium bowl, combine the coconut aminos, honey, orange juice, rice vinegar, ginger, sesame oil, garlic, and red pepper flakes. Whisk thoroughly to combine.

2. Transfer the sauce to a large skillet over medium heat and bring to a low simmer. Cook for 4 to 5 minutes, or until it begins to reduce.

3. Add the chicken and cook for 5 to 6 minutes, or until cooked through. Stir well to combine with the sauce.

4. Add the daikon noodles and toss well to combine, cooking for an additional 3 to 4 minutes, or until the noodles are tender.

5. Taste and season with salt and pepper, if necessary. Serve hot.

TIP: Use the gluten-free soy sauce if you aren't strict Paleo.

PER SERVING Calories: 438; Saturated Fat: 0g; Total Fat: 5g; Protein: 53g; Total Carbs: 44g; Fiber: 1g; Sodium: 267mg

Shredded Chicken and Cabbage Salad with Peanut Sauce

NO COOK • ONE POT • DAIRY-FREE • KETO

Cabbage is so easy to spiralize. I always forget about it because it doesn't actually yield noodles, but the spiralizer does a super-awesome job of quickly shredding it for me, saving me time and a huge mess in the kitchen. This salad is quick and light and full of flavor—just cabbage, chicken, and some fresh orange juice, with a little peanut vinaigrette to spice it up!

Serves 2
Prep time: 10 minutes
Blade: A

2 tablespoons freshly squeezed orange juice

2 tablespoons peanut butter

2 teaspoons gluten-free soy sauce

2 tablespoons rice vinegar

½ head cabbage, spiralized

1 large chicken breast, cooked and shredded

2 or 3 scallions, chopped

Salt

Freshly ground black pepper

Sesame seeds, for garnish

1. In a large bowl, whisk together the orange juice, peanut butter, soy sauce, and rice vinegar.

2. Add the cabbage and stir well to combine. Add the chicken and scallions and toss. Season with salt and pepper. Garnish with sesame seeds and serve immediately.

TIP: Use almond butter instead of peanut butter and coconut aminos instead of soy sauce to make this a Paleo recipe. Change this recipe up by varying the type of cabbage you use.

PER SERVING Calories: 295; Saturated Fat: 2g; Total Fat: 11g; Protein: 31g; Total Carbs: 17g; Fiber: 6g; Sodium: 543mg

Greek Salad with Cucumber Noodles and Chicken

KETO

One of my favorite lunches or light dinners is a big Greek salad with really herbaceous grilled chicken on top of it—the combination of spices with creamy feta and a nice tangy vinaigrette is fantastic, especially if you add crunchy cucumbers and salty olives. For this recipe, I spiralize the cucumbers and red onion, which adds a nice additional element of texture to all the chopped veggies and crisp romaine lettuce.

Serves 2 to 4
Prep time: 10 minutes
Cook time: 20 minutes
Blade: C

FOR THE CHICKEN

1 teaspoon salt
1 teaspoon garlic powder
1 teaspoon dried basil
1 teaspoon dried oregano
½ teaspoon freshly ground black pepper
½ teaspoon dried parsley
½ teaspoon dried rosemary
½ teaspoon dried dill
½ teaspoon dried thyme
2 tablespoons olive oil, plus more if needed
2 boneless chicken breasts

FOR THE GREEK SALAD

1 small head romaine lettuce, chopped
1 large cucumber, spiralized
½ red onion, spiralized
1 cup Kalamata olives
1 cup cherry tomatoes, halved
½ cup olive oil
Juice of 2 lemons, plus more if needed
1 cup crumbled feta cheese
Salt
Freshly ground black pepper

TO MAKE THE CHICKEN

1. Preheat the oven to 350°F.

2. In a small bowl, stir the salt, garlic powder, basil, oregano, pepper, parsley, rosemary, dill, and thyme together.

3. Heat a large skillet over medium-high heat. Pour the olive oil over the chicken, and season with half of the herb mix. Cook the chicken for 3 to 4 minutes per side until browned, then transfer to a baking sheet and bake for 10 to 12 minutes, or until the chicken is cooked through.

TO MAKE THE GREEK SALAD

1. While the chicken is baking, in a large bowl, combine the lettuce, cucumber noodles, onion, olives, and tomatoes. Toss everything together with the remaining herb mixture, olive oil, and lemon juice, then add the feta cheese and give it another good stir. Season with salt and pepper, and transfer to serving bowls or plates.

2. Slice or dice the chicken and top each salad with it. Taste and drizzle with a little more olive oil and lemon juice (if needed). Serve immediately.

TIP: Make this salad Paleo and dairy-free by skipping the cheese.

PER SERVING Calories: 1160; Saturated Fat: 97g; Total Fat: 23g; Protein: 55g; Total Carbs: 27g; Fiber: 7g; Sodium: 2693mg

Chicken Salad with Spiralized Carrots

5-INGREDIENT • NO COOK • ONE POT • DAIRY-FREE • PALEO

This chicken salad recipe is my go-to for meal prep when I want to have something easy to grab and serve over salads or with sliced cucumbers or even sweet potato chips. I like adding the spiralized carrots because it's a little different (chicken salad every week can get a little boring). Feel free to switch it up with any veggies you're trying to use up. I always try to sneak some extra vegetables into easy-to-make dishes like this one.

Serves 4
Prep time: 15 minutes
Blade: B

1 (12.5-ounce) can
chicken, drained

3 or 4 carrots, spiralized

½ cup mayonnaise

½ celery stalk, diced

½ cup grapes, finely chopped

1 or 2 scallions, thinly sliced

Salt

Freshly ground black pepper

In a large bowl, combine the chicken, carrot noodles, mayonnaise, celery, grapes, and scallions and mix everything together, stirring until combined. Season with salt and pepper. Serve immediately or refrigerate until ready to serve.

TIP: Make this a keto recipe by skipping the carrots and grapes and replacing with a lower-carb spiralized veggie like cucumber or zucchini.

PER SERVING Calories: 284; Saturated Fat: 2g; Total Fat: 13g; Protein: 27g; Total Carbs: 16g; Fiber: 2g; Sodium: 349mg

Chicken-Bacon-Ranch Wraps with Spiralized Veggies

5-INGREDIENT • NO COOK

This is a great meal-prep lunch idea—if you cook a bunch of bacon and chicken at once, you can wrap it up and save it in the refrigerator for recipes like this one. Chicken-Bacon-Ranch Wraps are super delicious, and adding spiralized veggies is such a great way to get even more vegetables into your diet. You can use gluten-free tortillas if you want, but big leaves of romaine or iceberg lettuce work wonderfully as well.

Serves 2
Prep time: 5 minutes
Blade: D

8 ounces cooked chicken breast, thinly sliced

4 cooked bacon slices

2 wraps of your choice—to keep Paleo, use lettuce, collard green leaves, or cabbage

2 or 3 carrots, spiralized

1 zucchini, spiralized

2 tablespoons your favorite ranch dressing

Sliced tomato or avocado (optional)

1. Assemble the wraps by layering the chicken and bacon within the lettuce or collard green leaves, followed by the carrot and zucchini noodles.

2. Drizzle with ranch dressing, add tomato or avocado (if using), and roll up. Enjoy immediately or store in the refrigerator for later.

TIP: Make these keto by adding the avocado, plus a slice of cheese for extra fat.

PER SERVING Calories: 562; Saturated Fat: 7g; Total Fat: 22g; Protein: 51g; Total Carbs: 38g; Fiber: 4g; Sodium: 1501mg

Turkey Zoodle Burgers

5-INGREDIENT • DAIRY-FREE • PALEO

I don't make turkey burgers very often because I find them to be a little too dry for my taste, but I like adding zucchini noodles to them, since they both add moisture and up the veggie content. I use the fettuccini blade and then give them a rough chop before adding them to the meat mixture.

Makes 4 burgers
Prep time: 10 minutes
Cook time: 15 minutes
Blade: B

1 pound ground turkey

1 large zucchini, spiralized

½ white onion, diced

1 large egg, beaten

1 garlic clove, minced

Salt

Freshly ground black pepper

1 or 2 tablespoons olive oil

Sliced tomatoes, lettuce, salad, or gluten-free buns, for serving (optional)

1. In a large bowl, combine the turkey, zucchini noodles, onion, egg, and garlic. Season with salt and pepper.

2. Mix well with your hands and divide into 4 equal sections, creating patties.

3. In a large skillet over medium heat, heat the olive oil. Cook the patties for 5 to 6 minutes per side, or until cooked completely through.

4. Serve hot with sliced tomato and lettuce, over a salad, or on a gluten-free bun.

TIP: Use beef or chicken instead of turkey if you feel like mixing it up.

PER SERVING Calories: 222; Saturated Fat: 2g; Total Fat: 11g; Protein: 29g; Total Carbs: 4g; Fiber: 1g; Sodium: 122mg

Chicken Pot Pie

DAIRY-FREE

This chicken pot pie uses spiralized potatoes as a top crust, which I like because it's fun and different, and it's so much faster than making a batch of mashed potatoes or pie crust to top the pie. And unlike most comfort foods, this recipe is ready in a flash.

Serves 4
Prep time: 5 minutes
Cook time: 25 minutes
Blade: B

3 tablespoons olive oil, divided

1 pound boneless chicken breast, diced

1 onion, spiralized and chopped

2 celery stalks, chopped

1 garlic clove, minced

2 carrots, spiralized and chopped

1 cup green peas (thawed if frozen)

Salt

Freshly ground black pepper

1 cup chicken broth

3 russet potatoes, spiralized

1. Preheat the oven to 400°F.

2. In a large skillet over medium heat, heat 1½ tablespoons of olive oil. Sauté the chicken, onion, celery, and garlic for 5 to 7 minutes, or until the chicken begins to brown slightly.

3. Add the carrots and peas, and season with salt and pepper. Stir everything together to combine. Add the chicken broth, and bring everything to a low simmer.

4. Transfer the mixture to a 9-by-13-inch baking dish.

5. In the same skillet over medium heat, sauté the potato noodles in the remaining 1½ tablespoons of olive oil for 2 to 3 minutes, or until tender. Season with salt and pepper.

6. Spread the potato noodles on top of the chicken mixture in the baking dish and gently press down on the noodles to form a crust. Bake for 10 to 15 minutes, or until golden brown, and serve.

TIP: If you aren't dairy-free, substitute heavy (whipping) cream for half of the chicken broth. Use sweet potatoes instead of russet to make this pot pie Paleo.

PER SERVING Calories: 431; Saturated Fat: 4g; Total Fat: 20g; Protein: 39g; Total Carbs: 37g; Fiber: 7g; Sodium: 368mg

Chicken and "Rice" Casserole

ONE POT • KETO

My husband and I lived in Minnesota for a while, and one of my favorite things about it was how cozy everyone got about food in the winter. Hot dish—another term for casseroles—was a huge thing, and it was the most delicious way to eat when there was snow falling outside. Of course, most of those recipes are super carb-heavy, but like with any other recipe, you can easily make substitutions. This chicken and "rice" casserole uses chopped up veggie noodles instead of rice, and you'll find that not only is it delicious, but it cooks a lot faster, too.

Serves 4 to 6
Prep time: 5 minutes
Cook time: 25 minutes
Blade: D

4 boneless chicken thighs, chopped or diced

2 tablespoons grass-fed butter, melted

Salt

Freshly ground black pepper

4 or 5 summer squash, spiralized and chopped into "rice"

1 onion, spiralized and chopped

1 garlic clove, minced

1 cup chicken broth

2 (10.5-ounce) cans condensed cream of mushroom soup

1. Preheat the oven to 375°F.

2. In a 9-by-13-inch baking dish, combine the chicken and melted butter and mix well. Season with salt and pepper.

3. Add the summer squash, onion, garlic, broth, and cream of mushroom soup. Season again with salt and pepper and stir well to combine, then cover the dish with aluminum foil.

4. Bake for 20 to 25 minutes, or until the chicken is cooked through and everything else is hot, and serve.

TIP: Use spiralized (or sliced/diced) potatoes if you aren't counting carbs and want a more traditional casserole dish— you may need to increase the baking time slightly.

PER SERVING Calories: 598; Saturated Fat: 13g; Total Fat: 41g; Protein: 37g; Total Carbs: 21g; Fiber: 3g; Sodium: 1384mg

Sweet Potato Noodle Taco Skillet

ONE POT · DAIRY-FREE · PALEO

Sometimes I crave the flavor of a taco salad but also want a hot meal for dinner, so I add sweet potato noodles to a pan of ground turkey to satisfy both cravings. The result is a delicious one-pot taco noodle skillet that I think you and your family will really love.

Serves 4
Prep time: 5 minutes
Cook time: 20 minutes
Blade: C

1 tablespoon olive oil

½ onion, diced

1 garlic clove, minced

Salt

Freshly ground black pepper

1 pound ground turkey

2 tablespoons taco seasoning

1 lime, plus lime wedges
for serving

2 medium sweet potatoes,
spiralized

¾ cup salsa, divided

1 avocado, diced, for serving

2 to 3 tablespoons chopped
fresh cilantro, for garnish

1. In a large skillet over medium heat, heat the olive oil. Sauté the onion and garlic for 2 to 3 minutes, or until the garlic is fragrant and the onion is softened slightly, stirring occasionally to keep the onion from sticking. Season with salt and pepper.

2. Add the ground turkey and taco seasoning to the skillet, and stir everything together. Cook for 5 to 7 minutes until browned.

3. Squeeze one lime over the turkey, and add the sweet potato noodles to the skillet. Season again with salt and pepper, and stir to combine, cooking for 4 to 5 more minutes until the noodles are fork-tender.

4. Pour about half of the salsa in and stir. Serve with lime wedges, the remaining salsa, avocado, and a sprinkle of cilantro.

TIP: If you aren't dairy-free, add some shredded cheese and sour cream as a topping.

PER SERVING Calories: 363; Saturated Fat: 3g; Total Fat: 16g; Protein: 29g; Total Carbs: 28g; Fiber: 6g; Sodium: 1058mg

Keto Chicken Parmesan over Zucchini Noodles

KETO

When I think of Italian comfort food, chicken Parmesan comes to mind right away. Unfortunately, it's loaded with carbs, so I like to make this grain-free version that swaps almond flour for bread crumbs and uses zoodles instead of regular pasta. The best part is how quickly it comes together. The chicken can be made ahead and refrigerated or frozen for even easier prep.

Serves 4
Prep time: 10 minutes
Cook time: 20 minutes
Blade: D

1 pound boneless chicken breast

Salt

Freshly ground black pepper

2 large eggs

3 tablespoons heavy (whipping) cream

2 cups almond flour

1 tablespoon dried oregano

1 tablespoon garlic powder

¼ cup olive oil

6 to 8 ounces mozzarella cheese (sliced or shredded)

2 or 3 large zucchini, spiralized

About 1 cup red sauce from Zucchini Spaghetti and Meatballs (page 116) or your favorite recipe

¼ cup Parmesan

1. Preheat the oven to 250°F.

2. Cut each chicken breast in half lengthwise, and use a meat mallet or a heavy skillet to flatten each piece—cover in plastic wrap and pound it vigorously until the chicken is as thin as possible. Season each piece of chicken with salt and pepper.

3. In a shallow dish, whisk the eggs and cream. In another shallow dish, combine the almond flour with the oregano and garlic powder, and season with lots of salt and pepper.

4. Dip each piece of chicken into the egg wash, then transfer it to the almond flour and dredge to cover both sides.

5. In a large skillet over medium-high heat, heat the olive oil. Carefully transfer the chicken to the pan and cook for about 5 minutes per side, or until the almond flour starts to turn golden brown. Remove from the skillet and place on a baking sheet.

6. Sprinkle the mozzarella over the chicken, transfer to the oven, and cook until the cheese is melted, about 7 minutes. Remove the baking sheet from the oven and sprinkle the Parmesan over the top of the chicken as desired.

7. In the same skillet, sauté the zucchini noodles over medium-high heat for 2 to 3 minutes until fork-tender.

8. Add the red sauce to the noodles and stir well to combine. Transfer the noodles onto serving plates, top with the chicken, and serve.

TIP: Make this recipe Paleo and dairy-free by skipping the mozzarella and using canned coconut milk instead of cream. Use a little extra red sauce if you want.

PER SERVING Calories: 635; Saturated Fat: 12g; Total Fat: 40g; Protein: 52g; Total Carbs: 21g; Fiber: 5g; Sodium: 770mg

Turkey Tetrazzini

KETO

This is a spiralized, keto-friendly take on a very carby, comfort-food classic. Turkey tetrazzini is a baked pasta dish loaded with sautéed mushrooms, creamy sauce, and egg noodles, so I like to make it with the ribbon noodle blade and use summer squash instead of pasta. The creamy sauce lends itself well to a keto recipe, so we skip the breadcrumbs on top and have a low-carb, high-fat dish that's as delicious as it is nostalgic!

Serves 4
Prep time: 5 minutes
Cook time: 25 minutes
Blade: A

4 tablespoons (½ stick) grass-fed butter, divided

10 ounces button or cremini mushrooms, sliced

1 garlic clove, minced

Salt

Freshly ground black pepper

2 cups cooked turkey, chopped or diced

1 cup green peas (thawed if frozen)

3 or 4 summer squash, spiralized

1½ cups heavy (whipping) cream

⅓ cup shredded Swiss cheese

⅔ cup grated Parmesan cheese

1. Preheat the oven to 375°F.

2. In a large skillet over medium-high heat, melt 2 tablespoons of butter. Sauté the mushrooms and garlic for 5 to 7 minutes, stirring occasionally, until browned.

3. Season with salt and pepper, remove from the heat, and use a slotted spoon to transfer the mushrooms to a 9-by-13-inch baking dish. Add the turkey and peas to the baking dish, and stir well to combine.

4. In the same skillet, sauté the summer squash noodles for 2 to 3 minutes until fork-tender. Season with salt and pepper and transfer to the baking dish, stirring gently to combine.

5. Add the remaining 2 tablespoons of butter and the cream to the skillet, and stir just until the butter melts. Pour the butter and cream over the turkey-pea-mushroom–veggie noodle mixture, and top with the Swiss cheese and Parmesan.

6. Bake for about 15 minutes, or until the cheese has melted and everything is warmed throughout. Allow to cool slightly before serving.

TIP: If you don't do dairy, make this a Paleo-friendly casserole by skipping the cheese and cream and using canned coconut milk. Add an extra garlic clove when sautéing the mushrooms, and season the casserole with salt and pepper accordingly—coconut cream tends to be a bit sweeter than dairy.

PER SERVING Calories: 703; Saturated Fat: 33g; Total Fat: 54g; Protein: 38g; Total Carbs: 19g; Fiber: 5g; Sodium: 440mg

Thanksgiving Leftovers Casserole

ONE POT

I don't know about you, but leftovers after Thanksgiving are one of my favorite things—for about 2 or 3 days, and then I start getting sick of them. This recipe can help you use up your Thanksgiving leftovers, or it can be a Thanksgiving-inspired dish to make any other time of the year. I like using any leftover veggies I have on hand, but I always spiralize a few carrots and onions because I tend to overbuy those and have them lying around.

Serves 4
Prep time: 5 minutes
Cook time: 25 minutes
Blade: C or D

1 or 2 cups chopped roasted turkey

2 or 3 carrots, spiralized

1 onion, spiralized

2 or 3 celery stalks, chopped

¾ cup chopped green beans

¼ cup mayonnaise

Salt

Freshly ground black pepper

1 or 2 cups mashed potatoes

¼ teaspoon paprika

1. Preheat the oven to 375°F.

2. In a 9-by-13-inch baking dish, mix the turkey, carrot noodles, onion, celery, green beans, and mayonnaise together. Season with salt and pepper.

3. Cover with the potatoes, and sprinkle with the paprika.

4. Bake for 20 to 25 minutes, or until warmed throughout. Serve hot.

TIP: Add any other leftovers you might have, like diced sweet potatoes or stuffing (although most stuffing recipes aren't gluten-free). Don't have leftover mashed potatoes? Try the spiralized potato noodle crust from the Chicken Pot Pie recipe (page 105) instead. And use sweet potatoes instead of white to make this casserole Paleo.

PER SERVING Calories: 315; Saturated Fat: 3g; Total Fat: 10g; Protein: 25g; Total Carbs: 32g; Fiber: 3g; Sodium: 511mg

Bánh Mì Lettuce Wraps, *page 114*

Beef & Pork Mains

Beef and pork are great protein choices—they're full of flavor and you can do so much with them, whether it's ground beef, pork chops, steaks, or ribs. This versatility means that I usually cook beef and/or pork at least twice a week, so these recipes are the ones I go back to over and over again. From meatballs to salads and even a lasagna-inspired dish, this chapter should keep you full and satisfied without extra carbs or sugar.

Bánh Mì Lettuce Wraps

DAIRY-FREE • PALEO

My first bánh mì experience was at a burger place called Beamers in my hometown of Roanoke, Virginia. It definitely wasn't a traditional bánh mì, which might be why I always get a little creative when it comes to working with these ingredients. These bánh mì lettuce wraps combine thinly sliced pork and all my favorite veggies (cucumber, radish, carrot) to make a delicious appetizer, snack, or light lunch.

Serves 4
Prep time: 20 minutes
Cook time: 10 minutes
Blade: D

¼ cup white vinegar, plus 1 teaspoon

1 tablespoon coconut aminos (or gluten-free soy sauce)

2 carrots, spiralized

½ spiralized cucumber

3 or 4 radishes, thinly sliced

2 tablespoons honey

1 tablespoon sesame oil

¼ teaspoon red pepper flakes

1 pound pork cutlets, cut thinly into bite-size pieces

4 to 6 lettuce boats—either romaine or butter lettuce, for serving

2 to 3 tablespoons chopped fresh cilantro, for garnish

1. In a small bowl, combine ¼ cup of white vinegar with the coconut aminos. Add the carrot and cucumber noodles, and radishes. Cover and set aside (or refrigerate for 1 hour; see tip).

2. In a large bowl, combine the honey, sesame oil, the remaining 1 teaspoon of vinegar, and the red pepper flakes. Add the pork and stir. Marinate for 10 minutes. (If you want, you can do this at the same time as the pickles and let the meat marinate for an hour as well.)

3. In a large skillet over medium-high heat, sauté the pork in the marinade for 5 to 7 minutes, or until the pork strips are cooked through.

4. Set up your lettuce wraps by laying out lettuce boats and filling them with cooked pork. Top with a generous serving of the vegetable noodles, garnish with the cilantro, and serve.

TIP: If I'm not in a rush, I like to do a quick pickle with the carrot, cucumber, and radish, so if you have extra time, mix up the veggies and refrigerate them for an hour for even more flavor.

PER SERVING Calories: 229; Saturated Fat: 2g; Total Fat: 8g; Protein: 26g; Total Carbs: 14g; Fiber: 1g; Sodium: 85mg

Vietnamese Noodle Salad

DAIRY-FREE • PALEO

One of my all-time favorite cuisines in the world is Vietnamese, and while I love a hot bowl of pho on a chilly day, there's nothing quite as refreshing as a chilled Vietnamese noodle salad on a hot one! My friend Corri and I used to go out for Vietnamese or order it in whenever we were hanging out in my backyard in Charlotte with our dogs, so anytime I have a salad like this I think of her. I decided to skip the rice noodles and spiralize as many of the veggies as possible to make this a grain-free, lower-carb, Paleo-friendly version of the Vietnamese noodle salad you may already know and love.

Serves 2 to 4
Prep time: 10 minutes
Cook time: 10 minutes
Blade: D

2 tablespoons sesame oil

1 pound thinly sliced pork

Salt

Freshly ground black pepper

2 carrots, spiralized

1 large cucumber, spiralized

1 large zucchini, spiralized

2 scallions, chopped

¼ cup rice vinegar

2 tablespoons fish sauce

1 garlic clove, minced

¼ teaspoon red pepper flakes

2 to 3 tablespoons chopped fresh cilantro

Lime wedges, for serving

2 to 3 tablespoons sliced almonds, for serving

1. In a large skillet over medium-high heat, heat the sesame oil. Sauté the pork for 5 to 6 minutes, or until cooked through. Season with salt and pepper and remove from the heat.

2. In a large bowl, combine the carrot, cucumber, and zucchini noodles, and the scallions.

3. In a small bowl, whisk together the rice vinegar, fish sauce, garlic, and red pepper flakes. Pour the dressing over the veggies and toss well to combine. Sprinkle with the cilantro, season with salt and pepper, and transfer to serving dishes.

4. Top with the cooked pork and serve with lime wedges and a sprinkle of sliced almonds.

TIP: If you aren't Paleo, try adding 1 cup of bean sprouts or using crushed peanuts instead of almonds.

PER SERVING Calories: 608; Saturated Fat: 2g; Total Fat: 28g; Protein: 69g; Total Carbs: 19g; Fiber: 5g; Sodium: 1448mg

Zucchini Spaghetti and Meatballs

DAIRY-FREE • PALEO

Zucchini noodles with meatballs might be one of the easiest ways to turn a recipe into a veggie noodle dish. It was one of my first veggie noodle experiences, and I will never get tired of eating this dish. Having a simple red sauce recipe that you can make anytime is so valuable—for this dish, browned meatballs finish cooking in the sauce and are paired with zoodles for a quick and easy Paleo dinner.

Serves 4
Prep time: 10 minutes
Cook time: 20 minutes
Blade: D

FOR THE MEATBALLS

1 pound ground beef

½ small white
onion, chopped

½ cup chopped fresh parsley

3 garlic cloves, minced

1 large egg, beaten

½ teaspoon dried basil

½ teaspoon dried oregano

½ teaspoon salt

½ teaspoon freshly ground
black pepper

1 to 2 tablespoons olive oil

FOR THE SAUCE AND ZOODLES

1 tablespoon olive oil

1 small white onion, chopped

2 garlic cloves, minced

1 (16- to 18-ounce) can or jar
diced tomatoes, with juice
(no sugar added)

½ to 1 teaspoon red
pepper flakes

3 or 4 large zucchini, spiralized

Salt

Freshly ground black pepper

1 tablespoon chopped fresh
parsley, for garnish

TO MAKE THE MEATBALLS

1. In a large bowl, combine the beef, onion, parsley, garlic, egg, basil, and oregano. Season with the salt and pepper and mix well. Roll into meatballs using your hands, then carefully add them to a large skillet over medium heat with the olive oil.

2. Brown the meatballs on all sides, turning every couple of minutes. Transfer the meatballs to a paper towel–lined plate and set aside.

TO MAKE THE SAUCE AND ZOODLES

1. In the same skillet over medium heat, heat the olive oil. Sauté the onion and garlic for 2 to 3 minutes, or until the garlic is fragrant and the onion is softened slightly.

2. Add the tomatoes with their juice and the red pepper flakes. Bring to a low simmer and add the meatballs back in. Cover and cook for another 5 to 7 minutes, or until the meatballs are cooked through.

3. Add the zucchini noodles to the skillet and toss gently to combine everything together. Remove from the heat, season with salt and pepper, and serve immediately, garnished with the parsley.

TIP: Add some grated Parmesan cheese to this dish as a topping if you aren't dairy-free or Paleo.

PER SERVING Calories: 546; Saturated Fat: 9g; Total Fat: 32g; Protein: 39g; Total Carbs: 31g; Fiber: 10g; Sodium: 466mg

"Pasta" Bolognese

KETO

One of my favorite things about experimenting with the keto diet is that dairy is no longer off-limits the way it is with most Paleo recipes. If you tolerate dairy, adding some heavy (whipping) cream or cheese to a low-carb recipe is such an easy way to make it much more satisfying, and this Bolognese sauce over zucchini noodles is no exception.

Serves 2 to 4
Prep time: 5 minutes
Cook time: 25 minutes
Blade: D

3 tablespoons
grass-fed butter

1 onion, chopped

2 or 3 garlic cloves, minced

2 to 4 carrots, chopped

2 or 3 celery stalks, chopped

1 pound ground beef
(preferably grass-fed)

Salt

Freshly ground black pepper

1 (16- to 18-ounce) can or jar
crushed tomatoes
(no sugar added)

1 cup heavy
(whipping) cream

Up to 1 cup water, if needed

1 tablespoon olive oil

3 or 4 large zucchini,
spiralized

Grated Parmesan cheese,
for serving

1. In a large saucepan medium heat, melt the butter. Sauté the onion, stirring frequently, until translucent and beginning to caramelize, 3 to 5 minutes. Add the garlic and stir well before adding the carrots and celery. Cook for another 3 to 5 minutes.

2. Move the sautéed vegetables to the edges of the pan, opening up a space in the center. Place the ground beef in the center of the pan, and mix it up. After about 3 minutes, when the beef is beginning to brown, start incorporating the vegetables into the beef, stirring everything together. Season with salt and pepper.

3. Add the tomatoes, stir, and bring the whole thing to a simmer before reducing the heat to low. Add the cream to the sauce, stir again, and allow to reduce for 10 to 15 minutes. If you want the sauce less thick, add up to 1 cup of water.

4. Meanwhile, in a large skillet over medium-high heat, heat the oil. Sauté the zucchini noodles for 3 to 4 minutes, or until fork-tender. Season with salt and pepper.

5. Transfer the noodles to plates or bowls, spoon the Bolognese over the top, and serve with Parmesan.

TIP: Easily make this recipe Paleo and dairy-free by skipping the heavy (whipping) cream and cheese. If it's too thick for your liking, you can add some chicken or beef broth to the sauce.

PER SERVING Calories: 1129; Saturated Fat: 46g; Total Fat: 85g; Protein: 56g; Total Carbs: 40g; Fiber: 10g; Sodium: 544mg

"Pasta" Carbonara

KETO

Spaghetti carbonara is one of those recipes that seems intimidating but is so easy to make for yourself, and it doesn't even require that many ingredients. The trick is to lower the heat before you add the eggs so you get a silky, sauce-like texture and not scrambled eggs. Don't forget the extra Parmesan cheese . . . that's what makes it extra tasty.

Serves 2 to 4
Prep time: 10 minutes
Cook time: 20 minutes
Blade: D

6 to 8 ounces diced pancetta

½ onion, diced

2 garlic cloves, minced

2 or 3 large zucchini, spiralized

Salt

Freshly ground black pepper

2 large eggs

½ cup grated Parmesan cheese, plus more for topping

Chopped fresh parsley, for garnish

1. In a large skillet over medium heat, cook the pancetta until it begins to crisp, about 5 minutes per side. Remove from the skillet with a slotted spoon, drain, and place on paper towels to keep it crisp. Add the onion and garlic to the skillet.

2. Add the zucchini noodles and sauté until tender, 4 to 5 minutes. Season with salt and pepper, and reduce the heat to low.

3. In a small bowl, beat the eggs and season with salt and pepper.

4. Slowly pour the egg mixture over the zucchini noodles, mixing or tossing constantly with a spoon or tongs as it cooks. (You want the mixture to become a creamy sauce that coats the noodles without the eggs scrambling.) Add the Parmesan and continue to stir.

5. To serve, transfer the zucchini noodles to bowls or plates and top with pancetta, more Parmesan, and a sprinkle of parsley.

TIP: If you can't find pancetta, you can always use chopped bacon.

PER SERVING Calories: 625; Saturated Fat: 18g; Total Fat: 47g; Protein: 42g; Total Carbs: 15g; Fiber: 4g; Sodium: 1617mg

Spicy Sausage Veggie Pasta in Garlic-Butter Sauce

ONE POT · KETO · PALEO

When I was a kid I never really liked sausage that much. My dad always liked spicy sausage in his pasta, but I just didn't appreciate it. Now, I can't get enough of it! I find it easy to cook, exceptionally delicious without having to season very much, and it goes well with any kind of pasta (or, in this case, veggie noodle). In this recipe, spicy sausage gets tossed together with veggie noodles and a simple garlic butter for an easy lunch or light dinner that's perfect anytime.

Serves 4
Prep time: 5 minutes
Cook time: 15 minutes
Blade: D

8 tablespoons (1 stick) grass-fed butter, divided

1 shallot, chopped

2 garlic cloves, minced

2 large zucchini, spiralized

2 or 3 summer squash, spiralized

2 carrots, spiralized

Salt

Freshly ground black pepper

1 pound spicy Italian sausage, cooked and sliced

1. In a large skillet over medium-high heat, melt 4 tablespoons of butter. Sauté the shallot and garlic together for 2 to 3 minutes, or until the garlic is fragrant and the shallot softens slightly.

2. Add the zucchini, summer squash, and carrot noodles and sauté for an additional 3 to 4 minutes until fork-tender. Season with salt and pepper, and stir in the remaining 4 tablespoons of butter.

3. Add the sausage and toss gently to combine, cooking for a few minutes more until everything is warmed through.

4. Remove from the heat and serve right away.

TIP: Skip the sausage and use about 10 ounces of sliced mushrooms to make this a vegetarian recipe.

PER SERVING Calories: 676; Saturated Fat: 28g; Total Fat: 59g; Protein: 22g; Total Carbs: 18g; Fiber: 5g; Sodium: 1090mg

Broccoli Rabe and Sausage Parsnip Noodles

ONE POT · DAIRY-FREE · PALEO

The first time I had broccoli rabe I was at a little Italian restaurant in Palo Alto, and I honestly didn't know what to expect. I ended up really liking it! Broccoli rabe is also sometimes referred to as rapini. It has broccoli-esque buds and somewhat bitter stems like broccoli, but it also has dark green leaves attached—kind of like a mix between broccoli and spinach. I love it paired with sausage, and for this recipe we sauté it all together with some parsnip noodles for even more veggie goodness.

Serves 4
Prep time: 5 minutes
Cook time: 20 minutes
Blade: D

About 1 pound broccoli rabe, stems trimmed

¼ cup olive oil

2 garlic cloves, minced

4 to 6 ounces spicy Italian sausage, casings removed, crumbled

2 large parsnips, peeled and spiralized

¼ teaspoon red pepper flakes

Salt

Freshly ground black pepper

1. Bring a large stockpot of salted water to a boil. Add the broccoli rabe and cook for 2 to 3 minutes, just until tender. Drain and set the broccoli rabe aside.

2. Return the pot to the stovetop and add the olive oil. Sauté the garlic over medium heat for 2 to 3 minutes, then add the sausage. Cook until browned, 5 to 7 minutes.

3. Add the parsnip noodles and cook for 3 to 4 minutes, or until softened.

4. Toss the broccoli rabe back in and stir everything together. Add the red pepper flakes and season with salt and pepper. Serve hot.

TIP: If you can't find broccoli rabe, you could use regular broccoli and add some mustard greens to take the place of the leafy bits and give that distinctive, slightly bitter flavor that makes broccoli rabe so good.

PER SERVING Calories: 486; Saturated Fat: 10g; Total Fat: 38g; Protein: 18g; Total Carbs: 20g; Fiber: 6g; Sodium: 708mg

Beef Stroganoff

ONE POT • KETO

I made a Paleo beef Stroganoff in another one of my books and used coconut milk, but this one is a keto-friendly recipe so we're using heavy (whipping) cream instead. I personally can't get enough of the combination of steak, onion, garlic, and lots of butter and cream—so incredibly indulgent—and with veggie noodles instead of pasta, I don't even have to think twice about it.

Serves 2 to 4
Prep time: 5 minutes
Cook time: 25 minutes
Blade: A

6 tablespoons (¾ stick) grass-fed butter, divided

1 large onion, thinly sliced

1 large carrot, spiralized

2 garlic cloves, minced

1½ pounds beef sirloin steak, cubed

Salt

Freshly ground black pepper

1 teaspoon thyme

1 cup beef broth

3 or 4 summer squash or zucchini, spiralized

½ cup heavy (whipping) cream

Fresh chives, for garnish

1. In a large skillet over medium heat, melt 2 tablespoons of butter. Sauté the onion, carrot, and garlic for about 5 minutes until the onion is tender. Melt another 2 tablespoons of butter in the skillet, and add the steak. Brown the meat on all sides, 5 to 6 minutes. Season with salt and pepper and add the thyme.

2. Add the broth and stir well to combine. Bring to a simmer and cook on low for about 10 minutes, or until the liquid has thickened a bit.

3. Add the squash noodles and cook for 2 to 3 minutes, or until fork-tender. Add the remaining 2 tablespoons of butter and the cream. Stir until melted and smooth, then transfer to serving bowls or plates and serve immediately, garnished with chives.

TIP: Make this a Paleo recipe by using unsweetened almond or coconut milk instead of heavy (whipping) cream; or just omit this ingredient entirely.

PER SERVING Calories: 1081; Saturated Fat: 36g; Total Fat: 72g; Protein: 87g; Total Carbs: 23g; Fiber: 6g; Sodium: 770mg

Beef Chow Mein

DAIRY-FREE • PALEO

This spiralized veggie chow mein is one of my go-tos when I'm in the mood for Chinese but don't want to wreck my diet by ordering takeout. Steak makes a great addition to this dish, but you could always use diced chicken breast instead. You can add almost any veggie you have that you need to get rid of, especially if it's a spiralizable one. The more noodles, the better, especially when it comes to Chinese flavors.

Serves 4
Prep time: 10 minutes
Cook time: 10 minutes
Blade: D

FOR THE SAUCE

¼ cup coconut aminos
(or gluten-free soy sauce)

3 tablespoons oyster sauce

2 teaspoons sesame oil

1 teaspoon honey

1 teaspoon rice vinegar

¼ teaspoon red pepper flakes

Salt

Freshly ground black pepper

FOR THE CHOW MEIN

2 tablespoons olive oil

½ pound thinly sliced steak

2 zucchini, spiralized

2 or 3 carrots, spiralized

½ cup shredded
Napa cabbage

2 garlic cloves, minced

½ teaspoon peeled minced
fresh ginger

2 or 3 scallions, chopped

Sesame seeds, for garnish

TO MAKE THE SAUCE

In a small bowl, whisk together the coconut aminos, oyster sauce, sesame oil, honey, rice vinegar, and red pepper flakes. Season with salt and pepper and set aside.

TO MAKE THE CHOW MEIN

1. In a large skillet over medium-high heat, heat the olive oil. Cook the steak for 4 to 5 minutes, or until browned. Add the zucchini and carrot noodles, cabbage, garlic, and ginger. Cook for another 2 to 3 minutes, and reduce the heat to medium-low.

2. Pour the sauce over everything and toss gently to combine. Remove from the heat and add the scallions. Divide among serving plates, top with sesame seeds, and serve.

TIP: Use shrimp instead of beef, or if you don't eat meat just skip it altogether.

PER SERVING Calories: 222; Saturated Fat: 1g; Total Fat: 12g; Protein: 15g; Total Carbs: 15g; Fiber: 3g; Sodium: 144mg

Spiralized "Jambalaya"

ONE POT · KETO · PALEO

I once made this recipe without spiralizing anything and served it over white rice, declaring that it was "gumbo." I was so surprised when the Southerners I served it to (mostly from Louisiana) quickly let me know it wasn't gumbo at all, because gumbo is made with a roux. Since I never cook with flour, I'm calling it Spiralized "Jambalaya" now. If I've learned anything from my time growing up in the South, it's that people are very serious about their regional dishes.

Serves 4
Prep time: 5 minutes
Cook time: 20 minutes
Blade: D

½ pound andouille sausage

1 tablespoon grass-fed butter

1 large onion, spiralized

1 green bell pepper, spiralized

2 celery stalks, chopped

Salt

Freshly ground black pepper

½ pound large shrimp, peeled and deveined

2 tablespoons Cajun seasoning

1 bay leaf

1 (14.5-ounce) can diced tomatoes (no sugar added), drained

2½ cups chicken broth

Chopped fresh parsley, for garnish

1. In a large stockpot over medium heat, cook the sausage until browned, 5 to 6 minutes, and set aside. Melt the butter in the pot and add the onion, bell pepper noodles, and celery. Season with salt and pepper. While the veggies sauté, slice the sausage into coins. Transfer back to the pot.

2. Cook everything together for another 3 to 4 minutes and then add the shrimp. Season with salt and pepper, then add the Cajun seasoning and bay leaf. Pour the drained tomatoes and chicken broth in, and bring the mixture to a low boil. Season with salt and pepper.

3. Simmer on low for at least 10 minutes. Remove the bay leaf and serve hot with a bit of parsley for garnish.

TIP: Use chicken instead of sausage if you don't eat pork, or double the shrimp.

PER SERVING Calories: 275; Saturated Fat: 5g; Total Fat: 11g; Protein: 29g; Total Carbs: 13g; Fiber: 3g; Sodium: 1016mg

Pork Fried "Rice"

ONE POT • PALEO

My brother and I always used to make fried rice together, and we still do sometimes, but these days we enjoy making this version that starts with daikon noodles, which are then chopped up or riced in a food processor. The daikon radish has a great flavor, and I'm always trying to find new ways to use it. I use pork in this recipe, but you can skip it if you want to make this vegetarian, or you can use chicken instead. Whatever you choose, it's going to be delicious!

Serves 2
Prep time: 10 minutes
Cook time: 20 minutes
Blade: D

1½ tablespoons sesame oil

4 to 6 ounces boneless pork loin, diced

About 1½ cups "riced" daikon—peel and spiralize the daikon and then either chop with a knife or pulse in a food processor until it's the consistency of rice

1 to 2 tablespoons grass-fed butter

1 garlic clove, minced

¼ teaspoon peeled minced fresh ginger

1 carrot, diced

¼ cup green peas (thawed if frozen)

¼ teaspoon red pepper flakes

2 tablespoons coconut aminos (or gluten-free soy sauce)

1 large egg

1. In a skillet over medium-high heat, heat the sesame oil. Sauté the pork for 5 to 7 minutes, or until browned and crispy. Remove from the skillet and set aside.

2. Add the daikon, spreading the "rice" out into one layer and letting it cook for a minute or two, then mix it up and repeat several times for 5 to 6 minutes, allowing it to get nice and crispy.

3. Add the butter, garlic, and ginger to the skillet, and stir well until incorporated. Add the carrot, peas, red pepper flakes, and coconut aminos.

4. Move all the contents of the skillet over to one side and crack in the egg, scrambling it right there in the skillet. Incorporate it into the rest of the fried rice ingredients and return the pork to the skillet. Cook for another minute or two, until it gets to your desired level of crispiness, maybe adding a bit more butter if desired. Serve hot.

TIP: Make this a vegetarian recipe by skipping the pork and adding another scrambled egg or two.

PER SERVING Calories: 402; Saturated Fat: 10g; Total Fat: 28g; Protein: 26g; Total Carbs: 14g; Fiber: 4g; Sodium: 446mg

Pork and Veggie Noodle Skillet

5-INGREDIENT · ONE POT · DAIRY-FREE · PALEO

This is one of those everything-in-the-refrigerator recipes that started out as a Sunday evening way to get rid of some leftovers but ended up being so good that now it's a recipe of its own. I love broccoli, carrots, and mushrooms together, and pork is always nice when combined with a bit of caramelized onion. It's a quick, one-pot dish that makes prep, cooking, and cleanup super easy.

Serves 4
Prep time: 10 minutes
Cook time: 20 minutes
Blade: A and D

1 or 2 tablespoons olive oil

1 onion, spiralized (blade D)

1 pound pork, diced

Salt

Freshly ground black pepper

10 ounces button or cremini mushrooms, sliced

1 head broccoli, florets removed and stem spiralized

2 or 3 carrots, spiralized

1. In a large skillet over medium heat, heat the olive oil. Sauté the onion for 2 to 3 minutes. Increase the heat to medium-high, add the pork, and cook until browned, 4 to 5 minutes. Season with salt and pepper.

2. Add the mushrooms and cook until browned, 3 to 4 minutes.

3. Add the broccoli florets and the broccoli and carrot noodles. Season again with salt and pepper. Cook everything, stirring frequently, for another 8 or 9 minutes until the noodles are tender. Remove from the heat and serve immediately

TIP: If you want to make this a keto recipe instead of a Paleo one, add ½ cup of heavy (whipping) cream before removing from the heat and top with ½ cup of shredded cheese before serving.

PER SERVING Calories: 260; Saturated Fat: 2g; Total Fat: 11g; Protein: 26g; Total Carbs: 16g; Fiber: 5g; Sodium: 406mg

Zucchini Noodle Lasagna Bake

ONE POT

This comforting casserole is a sped-up twist on a recipe I used to make where you use a veggie peeler to slice long sheets of zucchini like lasagna noodles. Now I use the ribbon noodle blade of the spiralizer, then toss everything together to speed up the cooking and baking time. It takes a little longer than any of the other recipes in the book, but it's worth it. Veggie noodle lasagna in 45 minutes? Let's do it.

Serves 4
Prep time: 5 minutes
Cook time: 40 minutes
Blade: A

1 tablespoon olive oil

½ pound spicy Italian sausage, casings removed, crumbled

½ pound ground beef

1 onion, spiralized

1 small green bell pepper, spiralized

1 (16-ounce) can tomato sauce (no sugar added)

2 tablespoons tomato paste

2 tablespoons chopped fresh parsley

1 tablespoon chopped fresh oregano

2 tablespoons chopped fresh basil

2 large zucchini, spiralized

8 ounces ricotta cheese

Salt

Freshly ground black pepper

½ cup shredded mozzarella cheese

1. Preheat the oven to 325°F.

2. In a large oven-safe skillet over medium heat, heat the olive oil. Cook the sausage until browned, 5 to 7 minutes, then remove from the skillet and set aside. Add the ground beef to the skillet. Cook for 5 minutes, using a wooden spoon to break up the beef. Add the onion and bell pepper noodles. Continue cooking until the beef is no longer pink, about 2 minutes more.

3. Stir in the tomato sauce, tomato paste, parsley, oregano, and basil. Once the sauce begins to boil, reduce the heat and allow to simmer for 10 minutes, stirring frequently. With 2 to 3 minutes to go, add the zucchini noodles and stir well. Stir in the reserved sausage and remove from the heat.

4. Add the ricotta, give everything a stir to combine, and then sprinkle with the mozzarella. Add salt and pepper to taste.

5. Cover with aluminum foil and bake for 15 minutes, or until the cheese has melted. Remove from the oven and allow to cool slightly before serving.

TIP: Make this a vegetarian recipe by using diced mushrooms instead of beef and sausage.

PER SERVING Calories: 335; Saturated Fat: 7g; Total Fat: 18g; Protein: 27g; Total Carbs: 19g; Fiber: 5g; Sodium: 911mg

Cheeseburger Noodle Skillet

ONE POT · KETO

When I started the keto diet, anything involving a cheeseburger became my favorite—I used to go to In-N-Out Burger for a 3x2 Protein Style (that's 3 beef patties and 2 slices of cheese with a lettuce wrap instead of a bun), and it was the best thing ever. I don't love doing lettuce-wrapped burgers at home, though, so that's where this cheeseburger noodle skillet comes in. Beef, cheese, a little tomato, and lots of veggies—pretty much the perfect keto dinner, and you can do it in one pot!

Serves 4
Prep time: 5 minutes
Cook time: 15 minutes
Blade: D

2 tablespoons olive oil

1 onion, spiralized

1 garlic clove, minced

1 pound ground beef

1 tablespoon tomato paste
or ketchup

Salt

Freshly ground pepper

2 large zucchini, spiralized

1 cup shredded
Cheddar cheese

1. In a large oven-safe skillet over medium-high heat, heat the olive oil. Sauté the onion and garlic for 2 to 3 minutes, or until the garlic is fragrant and the onion is softened slightly.

2. Add the beef and cook for 5 to 7 minutes, or until browned. Add the tomato paste and season with salt and pepper. Stir well to combine, and add the zucchini. Toss everything together and cover with the Cheddar.

3. Preheat the oven to broil.

4. Broil until the cheese has melted, 4 to 5 minutes. Cool slightly and serve.

TIP: If you aren't keto or counting carbs, use sweet potato or white potato noodles instead of zucchini.

PER SERVING Calories: 375; Saturated Fat: 10g; Total Fat: 25g; Protein: 32g; Total Carbs: 7g; Fiber: 2g; Sodium: 299mg

Resources

PRODUCE DELIVERY SERVICES

Farmbox Direct: Another wonderful produce delivery service that I've worked with in the past. You can do all fruit, all veggies, or a mix, and there are a variety of sizes and options to keep new vegetables in your refrigerator at all times. (farmboxdirect.com)

Green Bean Delivery: delivers to Missouri, Illinois, Indiana, Ohio, Kentucky, Tennessee. (greenbeandelivery.com)

Hungry Harvest: delivers to Maryland, DC, Northern Virginia, Philly, South New Jersey, South Florida and surrounding areas. (hungryharvest.net)

Imperfect Produce: A fruit and vegetable delivery service covering the West Coast (Los Angeles, CA; Orange County, CA; Portland, OR; Seattle, WA) and Chicago that saves "ugly" produce from going to waste. This is a great way to try new vegetables and experiment with your spiralizer while saving food and money. (imperfectproduce.com)

MY OTHER COOKBOOKS

- *The Big 10 Paleo Spiralizer Cookbook*: My second book, full of Paleo-friendly recipes and categorized by vegetable.

- *The Big 15 Paleo Cookbook*: My first book and a great one if you're interested in the Paleo diet.

- *The Big 15 Ketogenic Diet Cookbook*: This is my third book and is full of low-carb, high-fat recipes that are perfect if you're experimenting with ketosis.

OTHER SPIRALIZING COOKBOOKS

- *Zoodles Spiralizer Cookbook: A Vegetable Noodle and Pasta Cookbook* by Sonnet Lauberth

- *The Healthy Spiralizer Cookbook: Flavorful and Filling Salads, Soups, Suppers, and More for Low-Carb Living*

- *Spiralize It!* by Kenzie Swanhart

- *Inspiralized* by Ali Maffucci

Recipe Index

Index

Acknowledgments

I'd like to thank my amazing husband, Rob, who always supports me in my endeavors and believes in me to no end. Rob, you are the most wonderful person I know, and I feel so incredibly lucky to be building this life with you.

To my blog and cookbook readers, thank you as always for your support and excitement every time I come out with a new project. Almost five years ago I quit my job to work for myself and write every day, and none of it would be possible without you guys.

And last but certainly not least, many thanks go to Callisto Media for their continued partnership and the opportunity to work on another book.

About the Author

MEGAN FLYNN PETERSON is the writer behind *Freckled Italian*, a blog that focuses on life, love, and lots of food. Her previous cookbooks include *The Big 10 Paleo Spiralizer Cookbook*, *The Big 15 Ketogenic Diet Cookbook*, and *The Big 10 Paleo Cookbook*. She has called Virginia, Minnesota, and North Carolina home but currently resides in the San Francisco Bay Area with her family. You can read more from Megan at freckleditalian.com/blog, or find her on Instagram and Twitter @mflynnpete.